Hazel

God's Amazing Handmaiden

"...and on _my handmaidens_ I will pour out in those days of my spirit; and they shall _prophesy_."
Acts 2:17,18

"Verily, Verily, I say unto you, He that believeth on me, the works that I do shall he do also . . . because I go unto my Father."
John 14:12

Freddie Hightower Turner

Hazel

God's Amazing Handmaiden

Copyright © 1997
Freddie Hightower Turner
First Printing 1997

ISBN: 1-57502-639-2

Printed in the USA by

MORRIS PUBLISHING

3212 East Highway 30 • Kearney, NE 68847 • 1-800-650-7888

To Our Beloved Pastor

This Great Mother in Israel
So decreed by God's command,
Was a kind and loving shepherd
That stood with staff in hand.

The night was not too dark or cold
To search for one lost sheep,
'Til he was safe and sound within
She knew no restful sleep.

Our unselfish Pastor had
Such love for Jesus' name,
She had to share it with the world
Before He comes again.

It never grew too late
For one who needed prayer
Be it two or three a.m.
You'd always find her there.

This mighty woman of valor
Prophetess of the Lord,
Has fought the fight, kept the faith
Gone home for her reward.

By Freddie Turner

To
Her Children

Billie Jean and Delward Lee

and
Her Grandchildren

Cherryl, Sheila, Debbie,
Bobby, Gary, Mike, David, and Kevin

Owing a debt of gratitude,
we thank you for lending her to us!

Table of Contents

Acknowledgement

My thanks to my lovely Lord and His wonderful children for making this book possible.

Thank you, Rev. T.F. Tenny for your statement on the back cover. To her, you were "No. 1." She would be so pleased.

I am grateful to my pastor, Rev. Travis Sheppard, for his encouragement "just at the right time."

Barbara Means played a major role in the book. Barbara and her family shared many wonderful testimonies and she put the greater part on computer disk. Bro. Jim Vernon also spent hours putting it on disk. Sis. Lou Mattox typed and furnished testimonies and pictures.

Doris Berford, Pat Warren, and Bro. Mike Edmaiston helped "get it together." My beloved friend, Vivian, gave me a vote of confidence by asking for the first copy. My Aunt Gem Holt and my son-in-law, Joe Culp, gave me ideas. My daughter-in-law, Sheila Turner, ran numerous errands, took pictures, and typed it on disk.

I wish to thank Pastor Simpson's daughter, Billie Jean Clark, and granddaughter, Debbie Rose, for use of photos as well as Delward and Brenda Simpson.

I am indebted to June Basham and Debbie Walczak for use of their pictures and my Aunt Elzadah for her prayers.

I am grateful to my five children, Denzil, Vicky, Dale, Mark, and Cindy for their patience and help. My fine "little darlings" helped bring me back to the "real world" after hours of working on the book. Thanks Tiffany, Charity, Jonathan, Joshua, Justin, and Micah.

Last, but not least, Sis. Linda Cowan, my son, Dale, and son-in-law, Joe Culp for helping with the publication.

Preface

My life has been so touched by a most remarkable woman, Hazel Simpson, that I have never been the same. My gratitude demands that I write this book to share my joy with you. Her genuine love and true humility have left their perpetual mark upon my heart. She took credit for nothing but gave God the glory for everything - that is one of the things that made her great. This book is written to glorify God by making known His mighty acts in our present day.

She knew no prejudices. Race, creed, or color meant nothing to her. She only saw people as souls - souls that needed God.

Like Hannah, she prayed the prayer of faith that opened the barren womb; like Deborah, the prophetess, she arose a mother in Israel, judged God's people, and led them forth to joyous victory. Like all great heroes of faith, she was well aquainted with intercessory prayer and fasting. I am convinced she would have given her life for the truth of "One Lord, One Faith, One Baptism." (Ephesians 4:5)

The joy that permeated her being could have only been explained by the words of our Lord when He spoke of the living water that would flow from the believer. (John 7:37-39)

To know her was to love her, and I think you will see why as you read, *"HAZEL: God's Amazing Handmaiden."*

NOTE: Please keep in mind as you read the incredible testimonies within the leaves of this book that all are true accounts; however, try as we have to keep everything in sequence, we feel sure that there are some variations in the time frame.

Hazel Mabel Simpson
1915-1984

Chapter 1

CHILDHOOD DAYS

Zama, in central Mississippi, was such a beautiful community with it's farms nestled among the tall stately trees, the blue lakes and streams, the wildlife, and the gorgeous wildflowers sprinkled across the countryside. It was known as a "big sawmill town" in the early 1900's and often called "Frogtown" because there were so many frogs around the millpond. The men took sticks and killed them. Frogs legs were no rarity for supper in Zama.

Lafayette and Sally Sanders owned a large farmhouse which was used as a boardinghouse for men working at the sawmill. This community had its own logging train. The people rode the train into town to get the things they needed. The railroad track ran right in front of the Sanders' home.

Lafayette was a widower when he met the pretty widow Sarah, who was called Sally. They dated, fell in love, and married. This middle aged couple was blessed with a beautiful baby girl on August 17, 1915. They named her Hazel Mabel (pronounced "Maybell"). They were thrilled to have a baby girl, but she did not stay a baby long. She learned to swim almost as soon as she could walk. She brought a lot of sunshine to their lives. And you can be sure she never wanted for attention or anything else, for that matter!

Living on the farm was so much fun. She loved being outdoors where she could hear the birds sing and pick beautiful wildflowers. She made playhouses among the trees and pretended she was cooking like "Mommy." When she grew a little older, she spent hours cutting out paper dolls. This was one of her favorite pastimes. She was small for her age and looked like a doll herself. Her hair was long and beautiful.

One day she decided to cut her "bangs." She slipped into the back room, got the scissors, and began the task. When she had finished and discovered that she didn't like it, she decided to cut her bangs off. Her parents would never know. She cut it to the scalp! Then she was afraid, so she went and found a hat that would cover the front of her head. At the evening meal her father ask her to remove the hat. Hazel tried to talk him out of it, to no avail. "Young lady, remove that hat," her father said. Hazel was so embarrassed that she wouldn't go anywhere without that hat for a long time!

She always enjoyed watching her mother make homemade soap. Her Mom would put a fire under the big, black washpot, bring the lye water to a boil, add the meat scraps, and stir and cook until it reached the desired consistency. She would test it by running a feather through it.

Another thing that fascinated her was watching her mom turn cotton into thread. She would pick the seeds from the cotton, and use cotton cards to make the cotton into rolls. Then she held the rolls while it was spun by the spinning wheel into thread. It was fun to see how fast that spinning wheel turned!

There was no electricity on the farm. Kerosene lamps were used to light their home. She was glad when she was big enough to draw water from the well. Her Dad watched her while she turned the windlass that sent the rope into the well. When the bucket at the end of the rope filled with water, her Dad would help her draw it up.

One of her favorite times was when the peddler came by

her house driving his "rolling store." She gathered the eggs that the hens laid and exchanged them for candy and other goodies which she didn't have at home.

The day finally came when Hazel was old enough to go to school. She felt so big! She and her friends walked five miles up the railroad track to the one-room school house. Her Mom had packed her a good lunch. She thoroughly enjoyed her first day at school. She excelled in academics and loved sports very much. She usually won the footraces because she was the fastest runner in school.

Her personality won her many friends. She was never lonely. She and her friends would imagine they saw wild animals as they walked the railroad tracks. Her Dad would sit her down and reason with her to assure her that no wild animal would attack her. But when she was back with her friends, they imagined it again. It was fun!

Hazel's Mom dressed her in beautiful dresses that had been starched and ironed with the old smoothing iron. She always looked great. On cold winter days, not only did her mom dress her warmly, she had a nice hot meal prepared when she got home.

Pictured in the back right is Hazel as a little girl. The other children are unidentified.

In the evening the family would sit around the fireplace and eat popcorn or parched peanuts until it was time for evening prayer. Hazel would join her parents as they prayed and worshipped. Mr. Sanders was a Baptist deacon, who believed in living by the "good book."

These were days of spiritual awakening. The old farmers drove miles in their wagons to attend church. Although they worked long hard hours, there was always time to help their neighbors, to read the Bible, and to pray. They weren't in a hurry when it came to worshipping God either. The services were quite lengthy. Sometimes Hazel would fall asleep and her dad would carry her out in his arms.

The ladies gathered on one side of the church and the men on the other side for prayer before service began. Their intercessory prayer, adoration, and worship could be heard across the countryside. These old time Baptist and Methodist saints were not afraid to express their love for God. They shouted and praised God!

Then a mighty revival came to Zama. Hazel's parents took her to these meetings. She had never been to a church meeting like this before. These people were so happy. They had recieved the Holy Ghost like the disciples did on the Day of Pentecost. Needless to say, these people wanted to share this truth with everyone. They baptized just like the apostles - in Jesus' name. (Acts 2:38)

Hazel's Mom had been sick for some time, but when she was baptized, God healed her body. Once Hazel saw a little boy who had gotten hold of some kerosene, drank it, and turned blue. God instantly healed him when they prayed for him. (Mark 16:18) The many miracles Hazel saw as a child convinced her that God could do anything. She never doubted the power of the Almighty.

After Mr. Sanders received the Holy Spirit, he always stood and testified, referring to Nicodemus, the Jewish ruler who came to Jesus by night, inquiring what he must do to enter the Kingdom of God. Jesus replied, "Except a man be born of water and of the Spirit, he cannot enter into the Kingdom of God." (St. John 3:1-7) This became a joke to the youth of the church. They called him "Nicodemus." Hazel didn't like for them to tease and embarrass her about being Nicodemus' daughter. But there was no doubt, she loved her father. He always had time for her and often took her on his knee and reminded her of the goodness of God to their family. "We have always paid our tithes to God, Hazel, and though we are not rich people, we have never wanted for anything. There is something else I always want you to remember, a poor girl's name is all she has. The Bible says, 'A good name is rather to be chosen than great riches.' Don't ever lose your good name, Honey. The finest things in life are not bought with money."

Hazel and her friends liked to "play church" in the pine thicket near her home. She would find a tree stump and use it for a pulpit to "preach" to the other kids, but it was not all play. Hazel had found that an excellent place for an altar to talk to God when she was all alone. Once while she was praying, she saw a vision of Jesus on the Cross and felt the call of God on her life.

She knew that He was real; she had seen His mighty acts. She felt so honored that, at her young age, He would show her a vision of Himself hanging on the cross. She knew that sometime in the future, God wanted to use her to convey His message of Love to a lost world.

Hazel believed in speaking of those things which were not as though they were. (Romans 4:17)

God had called Abraham a father of many nations before it happened. He told Gideon that He had delivered the Midianites into his hand before the battle. (Judges 7:15) He also told Joshua that He had given Jericho into His hand before it came to pass.

Chapter 2

GROWING UP

By the time Hazel was twelve, she was driving the T-Model Ford. "Daddy's little girl" was beginning to grow up. She was helping with the cooking, house cleaning, and even learning to chop and pick cotton.

She enjoyed helping her Mom fix her favorite dishes to carry to the "all day singing" and "dinner on the ground" at the church. These were held often, and all the ladies and young girls had a chance to show their expertise at both cooking and sewing. They always wore their "Sunday Best," which often meant a new dress for the occasion. Folks would come for miles around to enjoy the fellowship.

Hazel's folks often invited the minister to their house on Sunday afternoon. Hazel helped with the fried chicken, banana pudding, and all the trimmings. She also helped by learning to milk the cows, to churn the milk to make buttermilk, and to take up the butter, molding it into square patties in the butter molds, and to do many other chores on the farm.

Hazel was very pretty and petite. Her long dark hair was naturally curly. She never lacked friends. They were just drawn to her. There was no doubt, she was destined to be a leader.

One day Hazel decided that she was old enough to have a grown up date. Of course her parents knew nothing about it. She went home with a girlfriend and arranged for her date to pick her up there. They went to the "picture show" as it was called in those days. Right in the middle of the show, in walked her Mom and said, "Young lady, you are going home with me!" Needless to say, Hazel never wanted to see her date again!

She had a close friend who was engaged to be married soon. In fact, her fiance` had already built their new home. This girl was beautiful, with one exception, she had crossed eyes. She was taking medication to correct this condition. The shots were hurting her badly, and she told Hazel, "If the next one hurts as badly as this one, it will kill me." She was right, the next one did killed her. Hazel was in shock. It was hard to believe her friend died so young.

Teenage years are difficult for most, and Hazel was no exception. She found herself right in the middle of those "turbulent" teenage years trying to find her place and, at the same time, testing her parents control.

In 1930 when Hazel turned fifteen, she found herself very much in love with Roy Simpson, one of her dad's employees. Roy was then in his twenties. They felt that they were meant for each other, so they decided to elope. Roy's brother, Cloice, had a T-Model Ford. They asked him to take them to Kosciusko, Mississippi. They were married there on the courthouse steps. They decided to keep their marriage a secret for awhile. After about six weeks, they decided to tell Hazel's parents. Mr. Sanders was "just devastated" at the thought of losing his "baby" girl. He took it so hard that they decided to live with him awhile. That while turned out to be three years.

On February 14, 1932, Roy and Hazel became the proud parents of a baby girl, Billie Jean. She was a beautiful baby who looked much like her seventeen-year-old Mom. The Sanders were just as proud to be grandparents. Now Papa Sanders had "two baby girls." It was almost more than he could bear when Roy announced, one year later, that they would be moving to Manilla, Arkansas. Tearfully, Mr. Sanders told Roy, "You are not going to take my babies away from me," knowing all the time, in his heart, that it must be. They were Roy's family; he must accept that. Lafayette and Sally Sanders waved goodbye to the little family. Hazel's childhood had come to an end.

Proverbs 31:10, 25-26

Who can find a virtuous woman? for her price is far above rubies. Strength and honour are her clothing; and she shall rejoice in time to come. She openeth her mouth with wisdom; and her tongue is the law of kindness.

Chapter 3

PRODICAL DAUGHTER

Manilla, Arkansas was "home" for Roy. He soon found employment. For Hazel, there were a few minor adjustments. Although homesick at first, she would make it just fine. In her mind's eye, she could see Mama Sanders walking down the long porch singing and her dad reading the Bible at the evening meal. Sure, she missed them, but it was time to grow up. She had her own family now. She had grown up!

She was an excellent wife and mother, putting herself into all that she did. She had learned responsibility growing up, and it just came natural for her to do her work well. She kept her home tidy and had nutritious meals ready to be served when Roy returned home from work.

When her work was done in the morning, she played with Billie Jean, just like her parents had done with her. Roy teased her about playing paper dolls after they were married and about riding in his red wagon! She didn't have to play paper dolls anymore. She had her own "live doll" to dress. She enjoyed every minute of it. Her family always looked nice.

In 1937, when Hazel was twenty-two, she became mother for a second time. This time it was a bouncing baby boy whom they named Delward Lee. He was a cute little guy and grew very fast. He didn't stay a baby very long.

Those were the years after the "depression," and the economy was still shaky. When Delward was old enough, Hazel took him to the field with her to pick cotton. This helped with the family income. Delward enjoyed riding on Mommy's cotton sack while she picked! She canned fruits and vegetables to assure that her family was fed well during the winter months. There was never an idle moment. These were happy days for the young mother except when the thunderclouds came. As a child, she was used to going to the storm cellars because there were many storms in central Mississippi. They had no storm cellar in Manilla, so she made her own by taking her children and crawling under the bed.

Billie Jean and Delward grew like "little weeds." Hazel had lots of fun with them because she was so young herself. They spent many happy hours playing together.

She wrote Mom and Dad back home and visited as often as she could. They were really special. They had given her such a wonderful childhood.

Billie Jean was doing well in school, and Hazel often recalled her own childhood days and those pretend animals. It seemed as if it were only yesterday.

World War II began, and Roy found employment at Fisher Aircraft in Memphis, Tennessee. The family moved to Memphis. This move would bring about great changes in their lifestyle. Hazel was a country girl. Those bright city lights looked so inviting. She was eager to find out more about city life. It was a brand new adventure for her.

Roy and Hazel started going to parties, and as usual, Hazel captivated those around her with her outgoing personality. She was the life of the party. Their many friends began to visit in the home. There was never a dull moment at the Simpson house. Friends found themselves quite at home.

Hazel found employment outside the home. She excelled in her job, and it was not long until she became president of a union. She remained an excellent homemaker and still gave her children special attention.

For social reasons, she joined a church that was compatible with her lifestyle. She was active in the church and liked by all the members, yet she knew in her heart that she wasn't right with God.

She was climbing the ladder of what the world called success. Her house was a hangout for their many friends, but she just wasn't happy. Her new lifestyle wasn't bringing her the fulfillment that she had anticipated. She found herself having to take tranquilizers just to make it through the day. This lifestyle was very demanding. That, she hadn't expected. There was just something missing in her life. What it was, she just couldn't put her finger on.

Her health began to fail and she wasn't even thirty years old yet! She was told that she must undergo surgery. While in the hospital, she made a vow to God that she would return to her childhood faith; however, when she recovered, she soon forgot her promise and returned to her old lifestyle. Adhesions grew in her side from the surgery. They caused her leg to jerk when she drove her car any distance. Her nerves grew steadily worse.

By this time, Billie Jean had become a beautiful young girl and married at fifteen, just as her Mom had done. When Hazel was in her early thirties, Billie Jean announced that she was going to be "grandma." Hazel looked more like a teenager, and her lifestyle was much the same.

She was told that she must have a hysterectomy. She entered Baptist Memorial Hospital for the surgery. Her Doctor was Dr. Ben Pentecost, President of the Baptist Hospital. He was an excellent surgeon. During this surgery something happened that changed the course of Hazel's life. She felt herself traveling down a long, dark passage. She knew that she was dying. Her soul cried out, "My God, have mercy on me, and I will live for you." The next day, Dr. Pentecost said, "Hazel, I would not have given a 'plug nickel' for your life."

"Doctor, God spared my life," she replied. Hazel had reached the lowest point in her life. Like the prodical son, she was turning her heart toward home. In her heart, she could hear the words of the old hymn:

> *"Coming home, coming home,*
> *Never more to roam,*
> *Open wide thine arms of love,*
> *Lord, I'm coming home."*

Luke 15:11-24

11) *A certain man had two sons:* (12) *And the younger of them said to his father, "Father, give me the portion of goods that falleth to me." And he divided unto them his living. (13) And not many days after the younger son gathered all together, and took his journey into a far country, and there wasted his substance with riotous living. (14) And when he had spent all, there arose a mighty famine in that land; and he began to be in want. (15) And he went and joined himself to a citizen of that country; and he sent him into his fields to feed swine. (16) And he would fain have filled his belly with the husks that the swine did eat: and no man gave unto him. (17) And when he came to himself, he said, ... (18) "I will arise and go to my Father, and will say unto him, "Father, I have sinned against Heaven, and before thee," ... (20) His Father saw him, and had compassion, and ran, and fell on his neck, and kissed him. (24) For this my son was dead, and is alive again; he was lost and is found.*

Chapter 4

RETURN OF THE PRODICAL DAUGHTER

*"Amazing Grace, how sweet the sound
that saved a wretch like me;
I once was lost but now I'm found
was Blind and now I see."*

Hazel had made a promise to God. She meant it from the bottom of her heart. As soon as she was able, she would keep that promise. Soon she returned home from the hospital. When she was able to be up, she contacted her next door neighbor and asked what time church services started. With great anticipation, she got ready for church that night. She really did not hear much of the sermon. There was one thing on her mind and that was her vow to God. As soon as the invitation was given, Hazel found herself in the altar crying tears of genuine repentance. She felt so clean. It was wonderful but she would not stop until she was filled with the Holy Ghost. It was promised, and she would not be denied. If Jesus' mother and the apostles had to have it, she must have it, too. And she would receive it! (Acts 1:14, Acts 2:38-39)

Her childhood vision of Jesus on the cross was becoming real to her again. Each night of the revival Hazel went to the altar to receive the Holy Ghost. Then one night, "it happened!" God's power flooded her soul. The heavenly wind of God's Spirit blew on her and shook her mightily as the most beautiful language she had ever heard proceeded from her lips! She had never felt anything so wonderful! It truly was joy unspeakable! What love the Father had bestowed upon her! She was born again of the spirit. She was a new creation, and her life would never be the same. She had gotten a drink of that living water Jesus spoke of to the woman at the well. (John 4:1-29, John 7:37-39) Hazel had been so sick. She never had dreamed that she would be so happy and feel such joy! There was no doubt she had found everything she had ever longed for. She would never thirst again.

Pastor McNatt asked, "You are still going to be baptized in 'Jesus' name, aren't you?

"Sure," said Hazel. If Cornelius' household (Acts 10:44-48) had to be baptized after they received the Holy Ghost, she would too. Hazel had been a chain smoker. When she was baptized the nicotine stains instantly left her fingers!

A few days later, it dawned on her that she was no longer sick. Lost in her new found joy, she had not noticed that her pain was gone! The adhesions in her side were also gone! She recalled how her mother had been healed of an abscess in her side and malaria chills when she was baptized in Jesus' name.

She spread the good news of her healing. "Good News" traveled fast! Her phone began to ring continuously. People were asking for prayer.

Her old friends just could not believe the change in Hazel. They predicted it would not last six months. The very thought of losing that joy frightened Hazel. She prayed, "Lord, just let me live for you, one day at a time."

While reading the bible one day, she found Hebrews 13:5, where Jesus said, *"I'll never leave thee nor forsake thee."* She was overjoyed when six months had passed and she was standing strong! She rejoiced when she read in II Corinthians 5:17 , *"Therefore if any man be in Christ, he is a new creature: old things are passed away; behold, all things are be-*

come new." She would never have to return to her old life. She had found a more excellent way. Nothing (except her own will) could separate her from the love of God, not even death. (Romans 8:38, Revelation 22:19)

She was very happy when she found Mark 16:17-18, *"And these signs shall follow them that believe; In my name shall they cast out devils; they shall speak with new tongues; They shall take up serpents; and if they drink any deadly thing, it shall not hurt them; they shall lay hands on the sick, and they shall recover."*

She was very zealous to work for the Lord. She asked Bro. McNatt, "Is there anything around the church I can do to help?" He told her that the baptismal robes needed to be washed. She was delighted to wash them and was soon asked to help in the office.

Once when she was returning home after helping with costumes for a play, a little boy ran right in front of her car. She was doing the speed limit and could not stop. She called on Jesus' name, and the car stopped. The boy had been knocked several feet, but he opened his eyes and said, "I'm sorry, I didn't see you." By that time his dad had arrived and began scolding him.

"Sir, don't scold him, just be thankful he is okay," she admonished. Hazel kept a close check on the boy. He suffered no harmful effects from the accident. Once again she saw what the mighty power of calling on the name of Jesus could do.

Pastor McNatt was taking pledges for missions one night. God spoke to Hazel to make a pledge. She didn't have the money, but she knew that she must obey. Roy did not share her new found joy and would not support the church. She decided to fast and pray that God would provide the money. After she had been fasting for five days, she was asked to pray for a girl who had epilepsy. When she laid hands on the girl and prayed for her, God healed her! Then she realized the real reason for the fast was for this girl. Jesus taught that some things are healed **only** by fasting and prayer. (Matthew 17:21) Not only did God provide the money, but He provided healing for this young lady.

The church was collecting clothing for the overseas missionaries. Hazel went to her closet and got some clothing that she didn't like very much. The Lord spoke to her, "Is that what you would give me?" Then she gladly gave some of her favorite dresses.

Hazel felt a strong desire to go to Columbia, South America, as a missionary, but she did not have the proper education required to go. She purposed in her heart, that since she couldn't go, she would support foreign missions to the max. She crocheted, cooked, made tissue flowers, and also took a job in the home of a Jewish doctor to support missions. The doctor listened intently as she witnessed to him about Jesus. When friends visited him, he always told them, "Mrs. Simpson is not a servant, she is a refined lady."

She started teaching a class of eight year old girls. She was very dedicated to her class. The girls loved her very much. Every girl in her class received the Holy Ghost and was baptized in Jesus' name except one whose parents did not attend church. When the parents would let her, she would go to the homes

Hazel Simpson and some of her eight-year old girls.

of some of the children to help get them ready for Sunday School.

She ran errands for the elderly. Often she sat in the waiting room at the doctor's office and crocheted. When someone asked her what she was making, it gave her a chance to witness for the Lord. That thrilled her so! Testifying of Jesus was her life and it mattered not to her race, creed, or color. **She only saw people as souls that needed a Saviour. She loved souls!**

She visited the hospitals and prayed for the sick; many people were healed. She was always in demand. People were always calling her for prayer.

One day when she was walking down the corridor of the hospital, she heard a young woman screaming. As she drew near, she saw this young woman flouncing all over the bed. She called to Hazel, "Come pray for me." Hazel walked into her room and began to pray. Instantly she was quiet. The nurses were amazed! She had failed to respond to the medication. They saw God instantly speak peace to her "troubled sea of pain."

It was there at the hospital that day that she met Cora Lassiter, who became one of her closest friends.

Roy was not too fond of Hazel's new life style. He chose not to go to church with her. He was working nights at Firestone Tire and Rubber Co. When Sunday morning came, he stayed home.

One day he and Hazel were out driving. They had the green light, when suddenly a car from the other direction ran the red light. It would have hit them had not the front end of their car stood up in the air! Roy began crying because he knew it had to have been divine intervention. Hazel often quoted Psalms 34:7; *"The angel of the Lord encampeth round about them that fear him, and delivereth them."* Now he had seen it first hand.

Hazel continued to pray for him. "Lord, you told the Philippian jailer that if he would believe, he would be saved and his house-hold," (Acts 16:25-33) "I want you to save my husband." Not only did she pray for him but she commanded satan to take his hands off him in Jesus' name.

It soon would be July and campmeeting time in Tennessee. Roy had caught his hand in an electric fan and cut it badly. Hazel prayed for him. God healed his hand. He decided to attend the campmeeting with her. It was there that he surrendered his life to God. His motto was: If you can't beat them, join them!

Delward had a wreck on his motorcycle and fractured his leg. Hazel had been attending a revival at Rev. Freddy Gray's church. She asked Delward to attend the revival with her and have his leg prayed for. At first he hesitated, but when she insisted, he decided to go. Two of his friends helped him walk, one on either side of him. He watched as people went up for prayer. When Bro. Gray prayed for them, they were "slain in the Spirit."

He told his friends, "When he prays for me, I won't fall like they do." Bro. Gray asked him if he believed in God and he said, "Yes."

Then Bro. Gray asked, "Do you believe God will heal you?" Delward believed God could heal but did not think God would heal him. When Bro. Gray prayed for him, he was also "slain" in the Spirit. He got up completely whole! In fact he went outside after church and out ran both boys who helped him to church! That healing made a believer of him. There was no way he could doubt!

Since Hazel was a Sunday school teacher, she felt condemned because there was a television set in her home. She felt it would be a stumbling block to others. She prayed and asked God to remove it from her home. One day when she came home, there was a delapidated car sitting in her driveway. She said, "Roy, there is an old car sitting in our driveway. Where did it come from?" Delward spoke up and said, "I traded the TV for it." Hazel started to open her mouth but the Lord checked her and said, "Don't say anything to him, you asked me to move it!" She said, "Thank you, Lord."

Proverbs 18:16 says, *"A man's gift maketh room for him, and bringeth him before great men."* Truly God had given Hazel a gift, and her gift was making room for itself. Little did she know that God was preparing her for a great ministry.

She learned to pray like Daniel and David. "Now I Lay Me Down to Sleep" prayers just didn't get results for her. She knew what the psalmist meant when he said, *"Evening, and morning, and at noon, will I pray, and CRY ALOUD; and he shall hear my voice."* Psalms 55:17. She agreed with James, that the effectual, fervent, prayer of a righteous man availeth much.

Her neighbors were not very fond of her praying. In fact, one man got up a petition to move her out of the neighborhood because of her prayers. "But when a man's ways please the Lord, He maketh even his enemies to be at peace with him." She did not have a thing to worry about. She just kept on praying. It was not long until that very man got sick and asked Hazel to pray for him. She was grateful to pray for him. She was a lady of great compassion.

One day her grandson, Mike came in the house crying, "Grandma, I've cut my hand." She looked, and it was bleeding. When she prayed for him, not only did the bleeding stop, but the gash closed, right before his eyes! Mike was amazed and so was Hazel.

Hazel developed a skin cancer on her right hand. Billie Jean had become a nurse and was quite concerned about it. Hazel felt sure God was going to heal her. She felt it was just a test of her faith because everytime she laid her hand on someone to pray for them, satan would say, "You don't have faith, just look at your hand." She ignored him and continued to believe God. One day she looked down at her hand; the cancer was gone! She did not even know when it left.

One day while Hazel was on a long fast, she was cooking for her family when all of a sudden she became very sick and felt as though she sould faint. Satan said, "You are going to die. She simply replied, "Goody, devil, I will just get to see Jesus sooner!" The sickness left and the sweetest taste came into her mouth. Such strength entered her body! She began to praise God for feeding her "heavenly manna." *Submit yourselves therefore to God. Resist the devil and he will flee from you.*

(James 4:7)

On another occasion, she was folding clothes for a sick lady when a spider bit her hand. She could feel the poison traveling up her arm. She washed the bite off with water from the water faucet in Jesus' Name. The lady was amazed that no harm came from the bite. Hazel remembered how Apostle Paul was bitten by a viper, shook it off, and felt no harm. She never believed in tempting God; however, she believed that when something accidently happened that God would allow no harm to come to her if she asked in faith.

By this time, Delward had grown up and joined the Air Force, but he had not forgotten his mother reading the Bible at the table and the teaching he got at home.

Just as surely as the prodigal son had returned home, so had Hazel. She had found the God of her childhood even more real than ever before. She loved walking and talking with Him. What sweet communion she enjoyed! It was wonderful to see His power manifested. She was so thankful that her children and grandchildren had seen what God could do. She would declare God's mighty acts to her generation. Never again would she be a prodical!

Roy and Hazel Simpson

Chapter 5

GOD CALLS HAZEL

One night, God spoke to Hazel in an audible voice. He spoke "Ezekial 3:17" three times. "Okay, Lord, I'll get up and see what it says," she replied. She read, *"Son of man, I make thee a watchman over the house of Israel: therefore hear the word at my mouth and give them warnings from me:"*

"But, Lord, I'm not a man," she said. He then spoke Galations 3:27-28 to her. *For as many of you as have been baptized into Christ have put on Christ. There is neither Jew nor Greek, there is neither bond nor free, there is neither male nor female: for ye are all one in Christ Jesus.* She felt so inadequate. Why did God want HER to preach? After all, she had not even finished high school. The spirit of the Lord came upon her and God said, "I'll be with your mouth."

Then she was reminded how Moses did not want to accept God's call (because he was slow of speech). *And Moses said unto the Lord, "O my Lord, I am not eloquent, neither heretofore, nor since thou hast spoken unto thy servant: but I am slow of speech, and of a slow tongue."*

And the Lord said unto him, "Who hath made a man's mouth . . . have not I the Lord? Now therefore go, and I will be with thy mouth, and teach what thou shalt say." (Exodus 4:10-12)

Accepting this call wasn't easy for her. Before her conversion, she had walked out of a church when a woman started to preach. She knew many people felt the same way, including ministers. It would be a "thorn" in her flesh, but she must obey God. It was such a wonderful life living for Him. She would take up her cross and follow Jesus. If the Lord told Apostle Paul, *"My grace is sufficient for thee: my strength is made perfect in weakness."* (II Corinthians 12:9) Hazel knew that He would do the same for her. She studied the Bible, and she would wake up with the chapters of God's word coming out of her mouth. She was an anointed evangelist and was very much in demand.

One night, when she first started her ministry, God gave her a message for a sinner. She noticed that there were no unsaved people present. She knew God had not made a mistake, but where was the sinner? At the close of the sermon as she was giving the invitation, in walked a sinner and knelt to pray! He had been listening outside!

Later, Hazel was asked to be assistant pastor for Bro. A.M. Launius. Together they saw God do many wonderful things.

Bro. Launius and Hazel were invited to preach a revival in Arkansas. Cora Lassiter accompanied them. She was a beautiful vocalist and a great prayer warrior. Together they made a great evangelistic team.

They saw the mighty power of God manifested during this revival meeting which was held outside. God confirmed His Word with signs, wonders, and miracles. (Hebrews 2:4) The greatest miracle was the harvest of souls that God gave. (Mark 16:20) There were many converts.

One night, when those "Big Arkansas" mosquitos were really bad, she noticed that even though folks were using repellent, they were being bitten. Then all of a sudden it dawned on her that not one had bitten her! That really built her faith.

God, who works in mysterious ways His wonders to perform, often uses natural occurrences to build faith for the supernatural miracles He wishes to perform. He was doing just that. For very soon a man came and asked Pastor Launius and Hazel to go and pray for his wife who was bedfast with cancer. She was in a coma. Her leg had already turned black. They left Cora in charge of the service. When they prayed for this lady, God healed her! She attended the rest of that revival! She was praising God for her healing! She and three of her children recieved the Holy Ghost. Her son is a preacher today.

The Willie Russom family had newborn twins, Gary and Jerry. Gary could not raise his head. James, the twins' older brother, told his mother if she would take Gary to church and have him prayed for that God would heal him. The pastor and Hazel anointed him with oil, laid hands on him, and prayed for him. (James 5:14) God healed him and he is preaching the gospel today in Japan!

Bro. Launius was asked to pray for a Mrs. Hollis whose face and hands were covered with skin cancers. God removed all the cancers. When her husband, who was crippled, saw that miracle, he sent for Bro. Launius to pray for him. God gave a message in tongues and interpretation through Hazel (I Corinthians 12:10) for Bro. Launius, "I will send my angel before thee." When he arrived, Mr. Hollis told him that he had just seen an angel. He had really been suffering. When God healed him, he stood on the floor and said, "This is the first time I have been able to feel the floor under my feet in twenty-one years. Praise the Lord!"

Bro. Launius preached Acts 2:38 in Hughes, Arkansas, at a Sunday afternoon meeting. God opened up the understanding of these people and as a result two whole churches were baptized in the name of the Lord Jesus. Bro. Junior Gonzales pastored one of the churches. When he and his church were baptized, the other pastor asked Brother Gonzales to baptize his church.

As an end result, thousands have been baptized because of this one service. The same Spirit that moved upon Apostle Peter at Pentecost, when three thousand were baptized, is still moving upon men today! These Spanish people found out that two thousand years later, God is pouring out that same Spirit on all flesh.

Pastor Launius and Hazel were asked to pray for Mrs. Alsup who had diabetes. She was blind and had both legs amputated. The doctor was concerned because she was not healing. The next week after prayer, the doctor was shocked at how fast she was healing. She did not have to use her blind tapes and records anymore. She could see!

A man, who was blind in one eye at Overton Crossing Church, asked for prayer. The Spirit of prophecy came upon Hazel and the Lord said, "In just a minute you will see." Sure enough, God healed that blind eye. First, he would cover one eye, then the other, and say to his wife, "Ruthie, I can see you out of this eye, and I can see you out of the other one."

When Pastor Launius was a young man, God had given him a vision of Hazel pastoring a church in Millington. He had never forgotten that vision. He kept it in his heart.

One night Hazel dreamed that she and the pastor were fishing. He was catching fish and she was taking them off the hook for him. Then she saw another pond with some large fish in it. God spoke to her and said, "I want you to catch these fish for me." She knew that it was time to move on. God had something else waiting for her.

She had prayed for God to provide a Jesus' name church for the young men stationed at nearby Millington Naval Air Base. She had driven the streets and cried and prayed for these young men many times. She had even talked to the elders about it, but they said, "It's just too hard a field. There have been MEN who went there and failed." But somehow she just could not get Millington off of her mind.

God always works on both ends of the line. In Millington, there was a couple who had been praying for seven years for a Jesus' name church to attend. They were Bro. and Sis. Ridley B. Durham. They had been attending a church of another faith.

One day Bro. Durham mentioned to a carpenter that he had been praying for someone to start a church in a vacant building on

Shelby Road. That carpenter just happened to be one of Hazel's converts! He was a young preacher by the name of Paul Patterson. He decided to start a church in that building. The building had formerly been used by personnel of the nearby gun powder manufacturer for a wash house.

Hazel pumped water with an old hand pump to clean the building and get it ready to be decorated. It really looked nice inside when Bro. Patterson painted it.

The first church located on Shelby Road.

The first service was a Saturday night singing in April 1957, with many area churches participating.

The crowd that gathered regularly began to grow. It was hot weather, and there was no air conditioning so the front doors were opened. Folks would even gather outside and listen. One night when Bro. Patterson was preaching a fiery sermon, a bug flew down his throat! Satan was not going to "bug" his sermon! He just kept right on preaching!

After pastoring the church several months, Bro. Patterson

decided it was God's will for Hazel to pastor the church. He recommended her to the church, and she was gladly accepted in January of 1958.

It was "love at first sight" with the church and Hazel. She asked Bro. Durham and Bro. C.E. McEntrye to assist her as deacons and Sis. McEntyre to be the youth director. Under Hazel's leadership, the church was blessed both spiritually and financially.

A man who lived near the old powder plant, by the name of Mr. Flynn, just couldn't believe the joy that Hazel manifested. He confessed, " I had to come several times to see if it was real. I have never seen such a happy woman in all my life."

God began to bless the youth under the direction of Sis. Wilma McEntrye. Two brothers, Roy and Benford Ross (who had been attending youth service in 1959), asked about getting prayer for their mother, Effie Ross, who lay on her deathbed, unable to get up or eat because of ulcers. She had been in and out of the hospital several times. The doctors had sent her home, saying there was nothing else they could do. Two-thirds of her stomach had been removed. One Sunday morning after service, Hazel and Sis. Bessie Durham followed the Ross brothers home and prayed for their mother. She began to get better. She could eat anything she wanted!

Hazel's first convert, Billy Watkins, had been a deacon of another faith who was amazed to see the mighty works of God. He was called to the evangelistic ministry. He often held revivals for her church.

Another young evangelist, Harold Smith, had come from Louisiana to hold a revival. He met Faye Simpson, Hazel's niece, at the revival, and it wasn't long before he married this beautiful dedicated young lady, and changed locations!

Two young evangelists, Bro. "Teddy" Ross and Bro. Junior Gonzales, also blessed the young church with their fiery preaching. Many souls were added to the church during these revivals and baptized at the old pond.

Roy felt it was God's will for Hazel to resign as pastor. When he could not be persuaded otherwise, she obeyed her husband. Her burden for Millington never ceased. She would come and peek through the window at the Sunday School attendance board to see now many were present. Her heart cried out for the church at Millington.

After several months, Hazel had a heart attack. She felt that she was out of the will of God. She asked God to spare her. She did not feel like she had won all the souls that she needed to win to stand before Him. "Lord, if you will spare me, I will go back to Millington and stay until you tell me to go," she prayed.

Roy was by her side when she returned to Millington. Bro. Billy Watkins and Bro. Harold Smith had both served as pastor while she was gone. She knew without a doubt that God had sent her back to Millington. It was so good to be home again where she belonged! She would continue "fishing" for the Lord and catch those "big fish" in her dream.

One day when Hazel was down praying, she was "lost in God's spirit." She heard the heavenly choir singing. The harmony was beautiful. It was many voices as one. Then it changed into the sound of a waterfall and finally into a voice. It was the kindest voice she had ever heard. She was sitting in a heavenly place in Christ Jesus (Ephesians 2:6).

Sis. Hazel Simpson baptizing in the early days at the old pond.

Mother Baker was an elderly blind lady who had served God faithfully many years. She came to visit Hazel one day. After she had gone through Hazel's house, she told her, "I have found your altar of prayer." Not only had this lady developed a keen sense of feeling in the natural, she had developed a sense of spiritual "feeling" that few know.

Hazel had dreamed of going to the Foreign Mission field. Now she realized Millington, Tennessee, was the mission field that God had called her to. She knew she was in the center of God's will because people came to Millington from all over the world.

One night Jean Parimore brought her two-year-old daughter, Diane, up for prayer. The doctor had said she must have a blood transfusion. She had only half-enough blood. Her hair and skin were almost as white as cotton. Immediately after prayer, her cheeks were rosy! God had instantly given her a blood transfusion. God was working through Hazel and confirming His Word with signs following. (Mark 16:20)

Hazel and Billie Jean took Mother Sanders to Mississippi to put flowers on Papa Sanders' grave. On the way home, they had a wreck. Billie Jean was expecting her third child. Her leg was broken and Mother Sanders had chest injuries. Hazel's nose was broken and twisted sideways. She also had internal injuries and a fractured leg. Mother Sanders and Billie Jean were hospitalized. Hazel asked God to not let her be admitted. Sure enough, there were not any beds left. God heard her prayer. The x-ray equipment was broken. Hazel pulled her nose around in Jesus' name and never felt any pain. She heard God speak to her in an audible voice, "I am the Lord that healeth thee."

Roy took her to the church and helped her inside. Sis. McEntyre was having youth service. She and the youth gathered around Hazel and prayed for her. Hazel stomped her leg as an act of faith. God instantly healed her leg. Her chest was still injured. The next night God healed her chest and she preached. One by one God healed every injury. The bleeding from her internal injuries stopped.

Mother Sanders condition grew worse. She had pneumonia. It looked as though she would die. God sent an angel into her hospital room and shortly therafter she was healed.

Pictured from left to right are Mother Sanders, Hazel, and Roy.

Pictured below from left to right are Gary, Bobby, and Mike, grandsons of Hazel and Roy. Picture was taken at the Memphis Zoo on July 8, 1960.

Billie Jean gave birth to her third child shortly after the accident. The wreck had not caused any complications at birth. First she had presented Hazel with Gary in 1947, Mike in 1949, and now it was Bobby.

Hazel was a proud grandma, and Roy thought it was special to have three grandsons.

Delward had

served his term in the Air Force, returned home, and married pretty Brenda Hayslip. In 1960, they presented these happy grandparents with their first baby girl, Cherryl, who looked much like her grandmother.

Once Hazel was asked to pray for a baby whose colon was too short. There was not an opening on the outside either. It would have to have surgery to extend the colon. She and Dolly Willingham prayed for the baby. After prayer, it only had to have the outside opening because God had extended the colon!

Lillie May Hollis asked Hazel to go to the hospital with her to pray for a distant relative, Shirley Tyler. She heard Shirley had undergone surgery for a brain tumor and had gone into a coma. Her condition was very critical. It had been 15-20 years since she had seen Shirley. When Lillie and Hazel arrived her grandmother said that Shirley's condition was still critical. Hazel walked over, leaned against the bed's siderail and gently took her hand and quietly prayed (under her breath). Suddenly, the girl began moving, opened her eyes, and called Lillie May's name. Lillie May wanted to be sure she was hearing correctly, so she said, "Who?" Shirley replied, "Lillie May," and began talking to them. God had instantly healed her.

Hazel was seeing a move of God in the church. She saw devils come out crying with loud voices, just as Philip saw in the Samaritan revival in Acts 8. The devil spoke through a young man and told her that he was going to destroy her church. She replied, "God's church is built upon the rock, and the gates of hell shall not prevail against it." He then told her that he was going to take her young people. She said, "Satan, you are a liar, and I plead the blood of Jesus against you." Then he said, "You can't cast me out, your master won't give you power." She replied, "He already did, Mark 16:17 says, 'In my name shall they cast out devils'." He said, "I'm not coming out! I'm not coming out!" Hazel replied, "Devil you are coming out of him in Jesus' name." The spirit was already outside the boy, but it was still saying, "I'm not coming out!" Hazel often used this example when explaining how the devil tries to bluff people. She always reminded the church that Jesus said that he (the devil) was a liar and the father of it. (John 8:44)

God blessed the church with a piano. Up until this time, Bro. Simpsons' tamborine and guitars provided the only music. The Lord sent not one, but two pianists. The music was an added blessing. There was a continual praise being offered to God. The people were so joyous and happy, and the church was experiencing a wonderful revival with Bro. Billy Watkins.

The revival continued into the new year of 1961. God was moving so mightily that the revival conntinued into February. Then on February 2, 1961, the church burned to the ground during the early morning hours. The Lord showed Hazel who set the fire and exactly where it was set. (I Corinthians 12:8) But she left vengence to God. Her faith never wavered. God was going to take a curse and turn it into a blessing.

Roy loved to tease Bro. Watkins about preaching the fiery revival that burned down the church!

Roy and Hazel Simpson

Chapter 6

HAZEL'S DREAM

"And we know that all things work together for good to them that love God, to them who are the called according to his purpose." (Romans 8:28)

Hazel's dream had always been to see God build a church that would bring Him honor and glory - one that would stand as a memorial to His great name. She was aware that "unless the Lord build the house, they labor in vain that build it." She joyfully served the Lord and had confidence that her dream some day would come true. She realized that dreams are not just magically borne on the wings of the wind; neither are they happenstance. They are a result of faith, careful planning, working toward a goal, and last but not least, waiting for due season. There is a season for every purpose under the sun.

The burning of the church building served only as a blessing to move "the Church" to the "heart" of Millington. Two weeks after the first church building burned, an old church building was rented from the Lions' Club with the option to buy. It was located across the street from the Strand Theatre, at Third and Wilkinsville Road. Since Millington was the home of the Memphis Naval Air Station, it was an excellent location for the service men who walked the streets of Millington. This was the first step in the right direction in the fulfillment of her dream.

She began to reflect on her life since she had known God. Reflection was a tremendous faith builder. She had received the baptism of the Holy Ghost in June of 1950. She began evangelizing in Mississippi, Arkansas, Louisiana, as well as Tennessee. God had done no less for her than he did for the apostles. *"And they went forth, and preached every where, the Lord working with them, and* **confirming the word with signs following** *. . ."* (Mark 16:20)

She never believed one should follow signs but knew first hand that **God confirms His Word with signs, wonders, miracles and divers gifts of the Holy Ghost**. (Hebrews 2:4) She had experienced this in her own ministry. No one could deny that. She cautioned people <u>not</u> to be a <u>follower</u> of signs but of <u>God's Word</u>. She said a person could be <u>healed</u> each time he is sick until Jesus returns and still not be <u>saved</u>. Salvation is the greatest miracle of

Second church building at Third and Wilkinsville

all. She pointed out that the man of sin (anitchrist) will have power to call fire down from Heaven and deceive people by those miracles which he has power to do. (Revelation 13:13-14, II Thessalonians 2:9-12)

Hazel was aware that many christians believe that they will be raptured before this time, but after much fasting, prayer, and studying God's Word, she could not see it any other way.

(Story Continued on Page 46)

HAZEL'S EXPLANATION ON TRIBULATIONS

Tribulation means great distress caused by oppression. Daniel 12:1, Matthew 24:21 says it's the greatest time of trouble ever known.

Revelation 12:6, God has prepared a place for the church where it will be fed during tribulation (1,260 days which correlates with Daniel's time, times, and the dividing of time or three and one-half years, Daniel 7:25, 12:7, and John's 42 months in Revelation 13:5).

Daniel was told it would take place at the time of the end (Daniel 12:9). The purpose is to purify God's people and make them white. It was not for the wicked. (Daniel 12:10) The wicked world never will be pure.

John saw a great multitude which no man could number which had come out of great tribulation and had washed their robes and made them white in the Blood of the Lamb. They were from all kindreds, tongues, and nations. (Revelation 7:9-17)

Matthew 24:24 says that false christs and false prophets will show great signs and wonders, and if it were possible, they would deceive the very elect.

Matthew 24:22 says, except those days be shortened, there should be no flesh saved, but for the elect's sake, those days shall be shortened. So, let's see who the elect are: [Christ has only one bride or elect (church).] (Rom. 2:28-29)

•Gentiles: Romans 15:9-13, John 10:16, Galatians 3:27-28, Ephesians 3:4-6, I Peter 1:1-2, Romans 8:33, Romans 2:28-29

•Jews: Romans 11:1, Romans 11:25-29, Isaiah 45:4, Romans 11:5,7

•Both: Ephesians 2:13-16, John 10:16, Galatians 3:27-28, Romans 2:28-29

So we see both Jew and Gentile are the elect and will go through the tribulation. Matthew 24:29-31 tells us immediately after the tribulation of those days shall the sun be darkened, and the moon shall not give her light, and the stars shall fall from heaven, and the powers of the heavens shall be shaken, and then shall appear the sign of the coming of the son of man in heaven . . . and he shall send his angels with the great sound of the trumpet, and they shall gather his elect from the four winds, from one end of heaven to the other.

The woman (church) who bore Jesus (Revelation 12:5-6) fled into the wilderness from the face of the great red dragon (Satan, Revelation 20:2) who had seven heads with ten horns with crowns on the horns. Let's see who the beast and false prophet are: (Daniel 7)

Daniel 7:23, the fourth beast is the fourth kingdom upon the earth. It had 10 horns (kings). There came forth a little horn (man of sin). (Daniel 7:20, Daniel 8:9-12)

This horn (man of sin) made war with the saints and prevailed against them until the ancient of the days (Lord) came. (Daniel 7:21-22)

He takes away the daily sacrifice (our right to worship) and sets up abomination that makes desolate (false worship order). (Daniel 12:11) This false one world system will last three and one-half years. (Daniel 7:25, Rev. 13:5)

II Thessalonians 2, Paul speaking of the rapture (Verse 1) continues in Verse 3, "Let no man deceive you for that day shall not come except there come a falling away first, and that man of sin be revealed. (Verse 4) Who exalteth himself above all that is called God or that is worshipped; so that he sitteth in the temple of God showing himself that he is God . . . (Verse 9) Even him whose coming is after the working of Satan with all power, and signs, and lying wonders. God will send strong delusion on those who love not the truth, and they will be deceived (Verses 11-12)."

Revelation 13:1 tells of the beast (kingdom) with 7 heads (mountains where she sits) and 10 horns (kings) with crowns. The dragon (devil) gave him his power, seat, and great authority. (Verse 2) He blasphemed God 42 months. (Verse 5) He made war with the saints to overcome them. Power is given him over all kindreds, tongues, and nations. He causeth all to receive a mark in their right hand or forehead that no man might buy or sell, save he that hath the mark, name, or number of his name which is the number of a man (666). (Verses 16-18) Notice 13:8 says, <u>all whose names are not written in the book of life will worship the beast</u>.

Revelation 17 tells more about this beast with 7 heads and 10 horns. Here we find the harlot or false church riding on the beast (kingdom). She is mystery Babylon the Great, the Mother of Harlots and Abominations of the Earth. Verse 4 describes the riches and color of the attire of her leaders. She is drunk on the blood of the saints and martyrs of Jesus. (Verse 6) Revelation 13:3 tells of a deadly wound she once received but it was healed and all the world wondered after the beast (except the elect). Revelation 17:9 says the seven heads are the seven mountains, on which the woman sitteth.

Revelation 11:3 speaks of two witnesses who prophesy 1,260 days clothed in sackcloth. Notice that is the same time God has prepared for the church which fled to the wilderness to be fed of God (Revelation 12:6). Revelation 11:4 says these two witnesses are the two <u>olive trees</u> and two <u>candlesticks standing before the God of the whole earth</u>. Compare this with Zechariah 4 where he saw the two olive trees one on each side of the golden candlestick. He asked the angel, "What are these, my Lord." The angel spoke of Zerubabel who would complete the present temple but was a signet (symbol or type) of Jesus (Haggai 2:23) building the spiritual temple. Haggai 2:4-9 says the latter temple will be more glorious than the former one which Zerrubabel completed. So it appears in Zechariah 4:6-7 the angel is telling Zechariah that the two witnesses are the Spirit-filled ones who come in under the grace dispensation or the latter temple or the Lord's church. Zechariah didn't understand and asks twice more. Then in Verse 14 the angel says these are the <u>two anointed ones who stand by the Lord of the whole earth</u>. Acts 10:38 says God <u>anointed</u> Jesus of Nazareth <u>with the Holy Ghost and with power</u>. So we see the Spirit of God anoints. Acts 1:8 says, "But ye shall receive power after that the Holy Ghost is come upon you and <u>ye shall be witnesses</u> unto me both in Jerusalem, and in all Judea, and in Samaria and unto the uttermost part of the earth. Romans 11:11-24 tells us the Jews and the Gentiles are the two olive trees. Israel was called the "nation born in a day" in 1948. (Isaiah 66:7-10) Hazel believed just as Israel was born naturally then, she will be born spiritually the same way. Romans 9:28 (speaking of the children of Israel) says, "For he (Lord) will finish the work and cut it short in righteousness: Because a short work will the Lord make upon the earth.   .

Hazel believed these two witnesses (Revelation 11) were Jew and Gentile believers in the Body of Christ. They are not left powerless against the signs and wonders of the antichrist. Daniel said they that do know their God shall be strong and do exploits (Daniel 11:32). They have the same power as Moses to turn waters to blood and smite the earth with plagues, and the same power as Elijah to shut the heavens that it rain not and fire proceedeth out of their mouth. (Revelation 11:4-7) Notice they finish their testimony before the beast makes war with them. The rapture takes place in Revelation 11:11-12. In Verse 13, the plagues or wrath of God is poured out on those who worshipped the beast. The wrath is much worse than the tribulation.

Men will seek death, but it will flee from them. (Revelations 9:6) For the destination of the great whore see Revelation 19:1-3, for the destination of the beast and false prophet see Revelation 19:20, and for the destination of the Church with its witnesses see Revelation 22 (Holy City).

Hazel did not believe the two witnesses (Revelation 11:7-9) were two individuals whose dead bodies would be in the streets at Jerusalem while the rest of the world viewed them on tv because the Lord was not crucified (Verse 8) in Sodom, Egypt, nor Jerusalem, rather he was crucified without the gate (Hebrews 13:12) of Jerusalem. Sodom and Egypt are a type of the sinful condition that will exist in all the cities of the earth at the time the witnesses are killed. Revelation 17:18 says it is Babylon "that great city that reigneth over the kings of the earth." (Elijah was the type of the raptured saint, and Moses was a type of the one that goes by the grave.)

* * * * * * *

She believed the same God that sent an angel and ravens to feed Elijah would provide for His children in bad times as well as in the good times according to Revelation 12:6, *"And the woman* (church) *fled into the wilderness, where she hath a place prepared of God, that they should feed her there a thousand, two hundred and threescore days* (42 months). " She often told the story of her friend, LaVelle Jewel, whose husband rejected her for her faith in Christ. One day he took her out in the country and said to her, "It's either that religion or me." She replied, "I'll never give God up." He pulled out a gun and proceeded to pull the trigger. To his amazement, the gun wouldn't fire.

She was left with twin sons, Billy and Bobby, to raise. She told Hazel, "You don't know how good it was to see God slow down a rabbit so your little boys could catch it for food."

One morning when there was no more food in the house, her sons came in and asked, "Mom, we're hungry; when are we going to eat?"

"Just in a little while," she replied as she entered her prayer closet to pray.

Her mother-in-law was there at the time. Soon there came a knock at the door. A man driving a pick-up truck began unloading groceries. "Don't accept these; they aren't yours," her mother-in-law said. "Oh! Yes, they are!" she replied. "God sent them." However, just to appease her mother-in-law, she called the local grocery stores; not one of them had sent out such an order. From that day forward, they never wanted for food again.

Today, Lavelle's twin sons pastor thriving churches.

Hazel had experienced such a move of God in the first building that burned. There were angelic visitations. She remembered when Cora Lassiter had made some slides at the church and an angel appeared in one of the slides. She had presented the slides during a service and invited visitors to come view them. It was no hoax. Hebrews 12:22-23, *"But ye are come unto mount Sion, and unto the city of the living God, the heavenly Jerusalem, and to an **innumerable company of Angels**. To the general assembly and church of the firstborn, which are written in* *heaven, and to God the Judge of all, and to the spirits of just men made perfect. "* Reflecting on past blessings gave her faith for future blessings.

Excitement filled the air as the people came up with new projects to make the money to buy this building. The people had a mind to work. Hazel and the Ladies Auxiliary made and sold chicken dinners each week to the local businesses. These dinners were very much in demand. Sometimes they got so many orders that they had to pray over the food and ask God to multiply it. He multiplied it many times, but it never ceased to amaze them each time God did it.

In 1960, Hazel was ordained a minister in the United Pentecostal Church.

In 1960, Hazel (pictured to the left and on page 48) attended an ordination service in Perryville, Tennessee, and was ordained a minister in the United Pentecostal Church.

The Tennessee District U.P.C. had given the church a loan of $450.00 which was promptly repaid. Bro. McNatt took pledges one Sunday night before he preached and about $2,000 was pledged. In just three short months the first down payment was made and the building at Third and Wilkinsville became property of The First Pentecostal Church of Millington, Tennessee, on May 4, 1961.

Roy was Sunday School superintendent. He had a God-given talent for getting people to come to church. Once in a Sunday School contest, he brought 50 people! The church began to grow. People were always getting "shipped out" and "shipped in" because this was military town. It took working to keep a steady number in the church.

Roy and Hazel went to the camp meeting, and Roy brought back a sign which read, "Surely God is in this place" and hung it across the front of the church. Visitors often acknowledged its authenticity.

The young ladies auxiliary of the church purchased an organ which greatly improved the music ministry of the church. Cora Lassiter directed the choir. The doors were left open in the summertime and the beautiful music and singing attracted the young servicemen. They began to find the house of God "a home away from home."

The church continued to be a staunch supporter of Foreign Missions. The missionaries were supported with prayer and correspondence as well.

Millington was not only a training base for "Uncle Sam," it was a "soul saving station" for Jesus Christ. Hazel taught the basics because she wanted her congregation to be established on a firm foundation of truth. Some of the military families had such a short time to learn basic truths before they would be shipped out or transferred to another base.

God blessed the church with young ministers who were "helps." (I Corinthians 12:28) It was exciting to see the Lord moving and saving souls, healing and blessing His people. He had added one hundred souls the first year.

That first year had been so fruitful. Hazel knew that she had climbed another step up the ladder to the fulfillment of her dream. Her heart was filled with gratitude. It was as if God had filled her cup and run it over!

> *"God is a Spirit: and they that worship him must worship him in spirit and in truth."*
>
> John 4:24

Chapter 7

MIRACLES PAVE THE WAY TO HAZEL'S DREAM

The young couples of the church were being blessed with babies. There was a young couple who felt "left out" because they couldn't have children. Roy and Evelyn Ross wanted a baby but Evelyn was barren, like Hannah of old. Hazel felt such compassion for her. She prayed that God would give her a child. Not only did the Lord bless this couple with one child, but He gave them three beautiful children. Hazel felt that she understood why Evelyn had been childless when in a few short years, God called her home. The Lord, who sees the end from the beginning, had it all under control. He gave Roy a wonderful wife to raise those three children. God is perfect and His ways are past finding out!

One day Hazel got a call from a man by the name of Mr. Bradley who lived in Memphis. "I've been confined to a wheelchair for five years," he said. "Do you believe God will heal me?" Hazel replied, "I not only believe He will, **I know** He will. Just come on out to service tonight, and we will anoint you with oil and pray for you like the Bible says to do in James 5:14." Mr. Bradley came that Wednesday night and God miraculously healed him.

Mr. Bradley's neighbors called Hazel. "Can you tell me what happened to Mr. Bradley? We have seen him pass our house for years in his motorized wheel chair, and now he is walking! What happened?" asked a pastor's wife (whose church believed healing ceased with the apostles). Hazel was delighted to explain that faith in the name of Jesus Christ had made this man whole just as it did the man at the Gate Beautiful in Jesus' day. She added, Jesus Christ is the same, yesterday, today, and forever. (Hebrews 13:8)

Brenda White, was a young lady who had also been raised to believe that God no longer healed. She had a young son, Van, who was a hemophiliac. They had nearly lost him on several occasions due to nose bleeds. She visited the church with relatives and was amazed at that little power-packed lady minister. She felt something different when Hazel quoted those scriptures. She had never felt anything like that in all her life. She could actually feel this power. She decided to have prayer for Van. God instantly healed him of the hemophilia! (He is in his thirties today and doing great. He gives God all the glory for his healing.)

A short time later, he fell out of a tree and broke his arm. You could see the bone protruding under the skin when Brenda brought him to church for prayer. God instantly healed that arm! He never had anymore problems with it.

Brenda had an affliction in her body, also. She became very weak. God showed Hazel that the affliction was serious and that they needed to fast. When they fasted, Brenda passed a growth that looked like a spider. She was frightened when she called Hazel and said, "I've passed something that looks like a spider, and I think I'm going to die." Hazel began to laugh and said, "No, honey, God has just removed that growth! You're healed!"

Even though God was confirming His Word with signs and wonders, Brenda still doubted Hazel's right to preach. She discussed this with Hazel and was told, "Honey, be careful because God might call you to preach. You see, I joined that same church you were raised in when I got away from home, and God still called me."

Six months later, Brenda was called to child evangelism and Van received the Holy Ghost under her ministry! She directed childrens' church and went on to become a great child evangelist. She also ministered in many jails.

Hazel and Brenda went to pray for an eight-year-old girl who was born deaf. The girl lived just across the Tennessee state line in Mississippi. God opened this little girl's ears. She had never talked but started making sounds. She was so happy that God healed her, she was trying to talk. She walked across the room and while her back was turned, Hazel asked, "Can you hear me?" The little girl ran and hugged Hazel! Hazel always gave God the glory. Isaiah 42:8 says, *"My glory will I not give to another."* She often said, "God can only use us if we stay humble before Him."

One night as Hazel was leaving church service, God spoke to her and said, "Son of man, go to the house of mourning." She did not know exactly what God meant, but she would find out. On her way home, she saw a building with a lot of cars parked around it. When she went inside, she heard a loud voice say, "Get that false prophetess out of here." She knew that she had found the right place. The voice was coming from a lady who had a microphone. Hazel inquired and found out that this lady had announced over the radio that she was going to die at 12 o'clock this very night. A crowd had gathered for the expected event. It was approaching 12 o'clock when Hazel arrived. She said, "In just a few minutes, we will see who the false prophetess is." The clock struck 12 o'clock, and the lady fell over like she was dead. Hazel walked up to her and said, "I command you to get up in the name of Jesus." She got up and said, "I want to wash your feet." Hazel replied, "This is not a footwashing time."

Hazel often used this example to teach people the difference between the Spirit of Truth and spirit of error, and to keep a proper balance. She explained, "People can be deceived if they don't know God's voice. Jesus taught that His sheep know His voice and a stranger's voice they will not follow." (St. John 10:4,5) **"That's why it is so important to know God's Word,"** she added. "You can go off the deep end if you don't know God's Word. Every spirit must agree with the Word."

Kathyrn Pafford (the church pianist) fell off a porch and broke her leg. She was a heavy lady. The doctor told her, "Mrs. Pafford, I can't assure you that you will ever walk again, but if you do, it will be nine months to a year." It was very depressing for her to sit in a wheel chair. Hazel encouraged her, "Now Kathyrn, you know God is a healer, and He will heal you if you just believe."

One night she wheeled up for prayer. While Hazel was praying for her, she was not aware that her hand had hit the lever on Kathyrn's wheel chair. Kathyrn thought that Hazel had purposely moved the lever for her to get up out of the wheel chair as an act of faith. Well, that is exactly what she did! God instantly healed her leg. She went back to the doctor. He looked at the x-ray and exclaimed, "It's healed, it's healed!"

About this time a man from Mississippi called Hazel. Here is his testimony in his own words. Bro. Robert Means is still in the Millington church today.

I was working on the boats on the river, and I was an alcoholic. One day when the boat docked in, I headed straight for a bar, as usual. I ordered a beer.

Robert Means

When I picked it up to drink it, something came all over me. I looked at the beer in my hand and thought, "there has to be a better life than this." I sat the beer down without even drinking it and walked outside. I looked in the sky and said, "God, HELP ME, and I will live for you."

I started going to different churches, but they didn't seem to believe all the things I read in the Bible.

A man that worked on the boats with me was Pentecostal and started witnessing to me about Jesus' name and the Holy Ghost. He told me about Sis. Simpson's church. I called her and asked her, "What are the qualifications for joining your church?"

She said, "We believe that you must be born again by repenting and being baptized in the name of Jesus for the remission of sins and receiving the gift of the Holy Ghost." This is what I had been reading in the Bible and what Bro. Dale McClure, the man who worked with me, had been telling me. I started going to her church when we docked in Memphis and started seeking the Holy Ghost.

I had stopped drinking but was still smoking. Bro. Dale told me I had to stop smoking if I wanted the Holy Ghost. When he said that, we were riding in a truck on the way to catch the boat at Helena, Arkansas, and I threw my cigarettes out the window. We prayed, and from that day on, I didn't desire a cigarette.

Sis. Simpson baptized me, and when I came out of the water, the nicotine stains on my fingers were gone. God also healed me of another condition that had caused me much pain when I did heavy work. I have done heavy work all the rest of my life and never had the problem again. Thank God!

I had read in the Bible where they called for the elders of the church to anoint with oil, and the sick were healed. I heard Sis. Simpson preach the same thing. I had three boys. My middle boy had knots all over his back. Sis. Simpson told me that God could heal him. I took him up for prayer and immediately he was healed! This gave me a lot of faith to believe for my baby son. He was born with club feet. He could not run and play with the other kids. He dragged his feet. I took him up for prayer. I was watching when the elders prayed for him. It was like the old timey 3-D movies. His legs went in and out and straightened! Today my son is 28 years old. His legs are still straight!

Soon after this, I got off the boat, after several months on the river, and found that my wife had taken my boys and left me. I would go to the church and lay on my face and pray for my boys.

One day Sis. Simpson told me, "Son, you just believe; you will see your boys again. I was praying for you and saw them coming to you, one at a time, the oldest one first."

In the years that followed, God gave me a Holy Ghost filled wife. She had four children and we had two more.

I didn't know where my boys were. We prayed for them all the time. Sis. Simpson's vision came true. One day, I got a phone call that my oldest boy, who was 11 years old, wanted to come and stay with me. They came to stay with me, one at a time, just like God showed her. When they came, each one was baptized and filled with the Holy Ghost.

When my middle boy, David, was 18 years old, he was in a terrible accident in Texas. He had just started working for an oil rig company. The big rig he was riding in had pulled off the shoulder of the road with a flat. A semi, coming down the road, ran into it. Three people were killed, and the rig that hit them melted to the pavement.

My other boy called me, "Daddy, you have to get here. They said David is dying. You and Mom are the only hope that he has (he meant God).

Sis. Simpson called before we left and told us. "Don't worry, David is going to be all right; I saw a speedy recovery, when I was praying." People in our church had started fasting and praying.

We drove all night. We would stop and call the hospital every hour or so. They would tell us he was still alive but hurry; he probably won't live until you get here. Immediately when we got there, they let us go into intensive care. They told us they didn't know why he was still alive. As fast as they gave him blood, he was losing it. They said, "He is in so much pain, but we have given him all the pain medicine, that we can." We prayed for him, and God touched him. They would let us go in to pray for him even when it wasn't time.

It would take too much time to tell all the things that were wrong when they operated, but God healed everything! In just a few weeks, he was out of the hospital. It is on the records that he is a living miracle. Today he is married and has two children.

The Curtis Gill family had been stationed in Millington. Curtis felt his need to be baptized in Jesus' name one cold winter's day. Hazel was sick. She tried to find another minister to baptize him, but to no avail. The pond was frozen over. "Lord, I'll baptize him if it costs me my life," she said. Curtis broke the ice with a stick, and she baptized him. The water felt warm to Curtis. That night, as Hazel raised her feet to get in bed, she felt something wrapped around her! God had put his invisible shield of protection around her. "Now, I know what protected the Hebrew children in the fiery furnace!" she exclaimed.

Curtis Gill's son, Bro. Don Gill, is now the pastor of Praise Tabernacle in Munford, Tennessee.

On another occasion when Jack Wilson was baptized at the same pond, several people present saw the geese "stand at attention" until Hazel had finished baptizing him. His son, Alan Wilson, now pastors in Olla, Louisiana.

The church was experiencing growing pains. Parking was becoming a problem. Some of the neighbors were not very happy about the music either. Therefore, they decided to get a petition against the church, but again, the Lord intervened and prevailed.

The church building needed to be remodeled and enlarged, but a city ordiance forbade it. As a result of prayer, the church was remodeled and eight Sunday school rooms were added as well as a baptistry and kitchen.

Hazel's ministry gifts were faith, healing, and the working of miracles. (I Corinthians 12:9-10) The other gifts of the Spirit operated through her when God chose. Her life was one of continual praise. She had a revival lifestyle. She often told her congregation, "Victory comes through PRAISE. If you want God to move for you, just praise Him!" It was normal for her to see God do the miraculous. The joy of the Lord was her strength.

In 1962, Billie Jean gave birth to her fouth child, David. Delward and Brenda presented Roy and Hazel with another granddaughter, Sheila.

Sheila was born with a deformity in her foot. The doctor told Delward that she would have to have two surgeries, and then wear corrective shoes. Delward told Hazel, "Mother, I'm going to have a little crippled girl." This so touched Hazel's heart. Hazel went to the hospital to pray for her. (She was only allowed to see her

Cherryl (left) and Sheila Simpson

through the nursery window.) As she stood there praying, Sheila's little crippled foot dropped down very quickly. When the doctor examined her foot again, he was amazed. It was perfectly normal as the other one. She is in her thirties now and has never had any problems with her foot. You could never convince her that Grandmother's God is not real.

Every Saturday morning, Hazel went out and invited people to Sunday School and church. Once when she was inviting a man to church, he asked her, "Where do you people get your baptism?" She was explaining when he said, "That name, that name! That's all you people study!" He put his hands around her throat. She said, "In the name of Jesus!" He walked away slinging his hands. Jesus had magnified His great name again! *"Neither is there salvation in any other: for there is none other name under heaven given among men, whereby we must be saved."* (Acts 4:12)

Hazel had visited and prayed for a very large family for some time. God had really laid a burden on her heart for the Forrest Warren family. Jeannie Hammontree, a daughter, came to a revival and recieved the Holy Ghost first. That started a chain reaction in the family.

One night when the invitation was given, an angel beckoned Mr. Warren to the altar. (Hebrew 12:22-23) He recieved the Holy Ghost. He was so happy that he became very anxious for his wife to recieve it. She teased him and said, "Now Daddy, don't forget the Lord had to come get you and take you to the altar." But it was not long until she experienced it for herself.

Soon most of the family were saved. What a revival! Three members of that family were called into the ministry. Jeannie, Woody (her husband), and Forrest Jr. Bro. Forrest Sr. became a deacon. He was a strong man of faith.

He had a brother named Rex. One Saturday morning while Hazel was parked in front of one of the members' house, Rex ran into the rear of her car.

She received whiplash in her neck and some dislocated vertebrae. Some folks thought she ought to sue, but she would not think of that. All she wanted was for his soul to be saved. She set aside a time every Sunday morning to pray for that family.

He, too, had a large family who did not attend church. God gave her about 16 members of that family. She was seeing a growth explosion.

Rex's son, Tommy, became a deacon and a man of prayer and dedication. One nephew preached and four granddaughters married preachers.

Woody and Jo Ann Hurt were a young service couple who had come to know the Lord in Millington. When Woody was "shipped out" and went aboard ship, he met Dave Shively. He witnessed to Dave, who was later sent to Millington. Dave found everything Woody had told him to be true and more. Dave's wife, Jan, brought the peanut brittle recipe to Millington. The church was truly blessed with the proceeds from this candy.

In 1964, Hazel became Grandma for the seventh time. Billie Jean gave birth to her fifth child, Debbie. (She resemble Hazel and her mom very much.)

Billie Jean's husband had been called into the ministry. Hazel felt so blessed to have her own family working for the Lord.

Jean May, the church organist, had her leg in a brace. God told her to take the brace off and walk around the church. Two young service men didn't understand what was going on. They proceeded to help her and to their great surprise the power of God moved them back! God healed her leg when she obeyed!

Bro Jim Basham entered the Veterns Hospital for tests. Something happened during these test, and he be-

Bro. Jim and Sis. June Basham

came unconscious. The doctors told his wife, June, that they did not expect him to live. The Lord told June on Saturday if she would ask the pastor and elders to go pray for him on Sunday that He would raise him up. The next day they went and prayed for him. After they prayed, the doctors went in and stayed a long time. When they came out, his doctor told her, "We don't know what happened, but he has made a turn for the better." But June knew what happened!

One Sunday morning, Sis. McEntrye felt a heart attack coming on. She got up and started for the altar. When she got there, she just fell over the altar and began to turn blue. Hazel and the church gathered around her and prayed for her. Needless to say, God healed her.

Wayne Grant, a young service man, had to wear thick glasses. God healed his eyes, and the optometrist said his vision was 20-20!

Hazel and some ladies from the church went to the general conference. The visibility was so bad that one could bearly see because of the fog. God made a path in the fog wide enough for them to see through. (This is a result of the gift of working of miracles found in I Corinthians 12:10.)

In 1967, Frankie and Carolyn Hegwood who had been stationed in Quonset Point, Rhode Island, were sent to Millington. Carolyn came from a holiness background. As they passed the church going to the drive-in movie theatre, she saw the ladies going in the church and conviction gripped her heart so much she did not enjoy the movie. They began to visit the church.

One cold December night in 1968, when Bro. Silas Petigo was holding a revival, they both were baptized in Jesus' name and received the Holy Ghost. This couple proved to be a real blessing. Carolyn was so talented. She had a beautiful voice. Frankie had a real zeal to tell the world about Jesus' love. He worked with the teenage boys and taught them to witness for the Lord. Later he became a deacon.

Steve and Veneda Nichelson, from Iuka, Mississippi, visited

the church. Veneda was baptized by Hazel. They now pastor a lovely church in Iuka.

Hazel's daughter-in-law, Brenda, had been under a doctor's care for anemia. The doctor said her blood count was so low that she must take one iron shot a week for seven weeks. She had not told Hazel because she did not want to bother her. While Hazel was praying, God showed her that Brenda was sick. She called Brenda and told her. Brenda said, "That's right. I have been so weak that I have had to rest when I vacuumed."

When Hazel prayed for her, God healed her. She was thankful that God was so mindful of her to show Hazel her affliction.

In April of 1969, the church at Third and Wilkinsville was paid for in full, but the Church had outgrown the building and badly needed parking space.

Dolly Willingham, the Ladies Auxilary leader, felt a call on her life. God was sending her to the black community. Hazel told Dolly, "You are one of those 'big fish' that I saw in my dream." This was the beginning of the outreach ministries of the church. She founded a church in Atoka, Tennessee.

Dolly recalled how her husband would not come to church with her at first. She had been so burdened for him because he had already had three heart attacks and was on blood thinner. She continued to pray for him. One day Hazel and she anointed his shoes and prayed God would direct his steps. The next Sunday morning during worship service, he walked in – IN THOSE SHOES! (He later became a deacon in the church.)

About this time another young lady came in the church that was near the Strand Theatre. Sis. Barbara Blevins (now Sis. Robert Means). Here is her testimony in her own words.

> My life was a wreck when I came to the Lord. I was driving around one Sunday just to try to get away from all my problems. I drove by the church and saw all the people going in the building. They looked so holy and happy. My heart just ached for

that same happiness.

I came back and went inside. I can hardly describe how I felt. When it came time for altar call, a prophesy was given out in tongues and interpretation.

No one knew me or anything about me. I had been praying at home, telling God, "Please, I don't care if I have to live in a shack, let me have a happy home."

I will never forget the message that came forth. The Lord said, "Seek, ye not happiness, but seek ye first the kingdom of God and His righteousness, and all these things shall be added unto you."

I ran to the altar with the secrets of my heart made manifest by God. (I Corinthians 14:25)

I told the Lord I would live for Him, happiness, or not. I felt so ashamed that I had left God out of my life.

Can you imagine how I felt, when I really started studying the Bible and found that prophecy in Matthew 6:33? To know that the mighty God Himself had spoken my thoughts!

I just drank in the testimonies that people gave of healing and deliverance. The first healing miracle in my life happened when I was very new in the Lord. I had an old baby stroller that I had repaired myself with some long screws, and they were sticking out. It was a nice day, so I had walked to church, and when I came home, the stroller tipped over on the front step of my house. One of the long screws went into my daughter's forehead. It made a large hole and was bleeding. I got in the car and quickly drove back to the church. I was young and scared. I ran inside the church; Sis. Simpson and Sis. Durham were still there. They prayed for her, and in front of our eyes, the hole closed up - the blood was even gone! It never mattered to me in following years, if people wanted some proof, I never forgot that. It gave me faith to always know that God could do anything.

Many other healings and miracles happened in our lives. I came to the church with a ruined life. The Lord gave me a new life and a Christian husband. Between us, we have raised 11 children. So you know there was always something happening!

When one of my sons was about five years old, our hot water heater quit working. We heated water on the stove to pour in the bathtub. I was carrying the water down the hall when Ben came playing and ran into me. All of the boiling water poured on him. It went on the side of his face and down the front of his chest. It was awful. I ran and called Sis. Simpson. He was screaming and crying. She came straight to our house. The minute she put her hands on him to pray for him, he stopped crying. She said, "God took the pain, and he will heal the burn." But the burn was still there! He got down and played with that awful looking burn still the same. I just couldn't understand, but I really believed God.

My grandfather died, and we had to go out of town to the funeral. I covered the burn all down his chest with a large bandage, and put a large loose shirt on him. Of course, my relatives wanted to see this. I got all kinds of advice on what to put on it and how infected it could get. I was just simple enough to tell them that I knew God was going to heal him. The next day when we got home, there was all new skin there! He was completely healed. My relatives have never forgotten that. God wanted to get the glory by taking the pain, but leaving the burn. If I had told them how God had healed it instantly, they would not have seen it for themselves!

Carrie Blevins

**Robert and
Barbara Means**

Dougie Blevins

Ben Blevins

When my daughter, Carrie (who is now 24 years old), was two, she was playing with some children. Our church at that time had a heavy metal door. They were playing after church, and someone slammed her finger in the door. The end of her finger from the first knuckle was severed at an angle. Bro. Richard Berford (who is a minister today) carried her to me with the end of her finger in his handkerchief. I took her to the doctor, and he stitched it back on. He told me that it would either take itself back, or turn black and they would have to remove it.

It never ceases to amaze me about the perfect plan of God. I was a single parent at the time, and my Dad and sister were coming from Michigan the next day to take me to my hometown to visit for a few weeks. The doctor said, "Well, I'll give you the records, and as soon as you get there, take her to a doctor. We don't want it to get infected."

There was much to-do from my concerned Mom and Dad over their grandbaby. The day after we got there, they took me to their family physician. The finger looked awful. My sister, who did not live for the Lord, was with me. We watched the doctor remove the stitches and throw the end of her finger in the trash can. He cleaned it, bandaged it, and told me to be sure to change the bandages to keep it clean.

My girlfriend wanted my kids to spend the night with her kids because they hadn't seen them in so long. She said, "Don't worry, I'll change the bandage." That night she called me at my parents house. "Barb, I thought you said Carrie's finger was cut off on the end. There is a whole finger!" You talk about shouting. It was just almost unbelievable. My Mom was in the church at that time, but my Dad

wasn't and my sisters weren't. I know now that
God did that miracle for them to see. No one could
ever come and tell them it wasn't true! My Dad is in
church today, and two of my sisters!

Lots of times, God uses miracles to save people.
My Aunt, who lived in Selmer, Tennessee, got cancer. She knew we really believed in healing. She called
me and wanted Sis. Simpson to pray for her. She got
the Holy Ghost and lived for the Lord for almost two
years after that! She died speaking in tongues. On
her tombstone today, it says, *"And whosoever liveth
and believeth in me shall never die..."* (John 11:26)

Debbie, Hazel's youngest granddaughter, had a tooth ache due
to dental work and was in a lot of pain. When Grandmother prayed
for her the pain stopped. Grandmother's God surely answered
prayer. Her grandchildren knew who to call on when they needed
help.

Hazel was ask to pray for a 24-year-old woman who had
cancer. Hazel told this young Baptist mother, "Honey, if you
can believe the stripes were put on Jesus' back for your healing, God will heal you." She replied, "I have to believe. I
have little children that need me." God healed her and she was
dismissed from the hospital.

Hazel prayed for an elderly lady in the hospital who had a
broken hip. When she returned to see the lady, she had been
dismissed!

Shirley Armstrong, Forrest Warren's daughter, had been di-
agnosed with a brain tumor. Hazel went to the hospital and
prayed for her. She had already been scheduled for surgery.
When they did the surgery, the tumor was gone. The only evidence that there had been a tumor was a scar where the tumor
had been. God healed her! To God be the glory!

Bro. McEntyre, a deacon, was driving along Thomas Street in
Memphis when a car driving about 60 mph on wet pavement
started doing tail spins, hit his car, and totaled both cars. His sister's

knee was injured. They were taken to the hospital, treated, and released. He could not walk without help. Two of the men helped him up the steps to the church. Hazel and Bro.Watkins prayed for him. God healed his leg. He had no need for help down the steps after service! It was wonderful to feel the healing virtue.

Bro. McEntyre was awakened one night by the voice of the Lord telling him to pray for Woody Hammondtree, one of the young ministers of the church. Woody and Bro. Watkins were driving a gas truck. He felt that praying for Woody while lying in bed would be sufficient, but the Lord impressed him to get up right then and pray for Woody. He looked at the clock and noticed the time. The next time he went to church, Woody asked, "Did you pray for me at such a time?" Bro. McEntyre replied, "Yes." Woody continued, "Well, I had gone to sleep at the wheel and headed down an embankment when I saw you and heard you praying and woke up just in time to stop! I appreciate your prayers. I pulled off the road and told Bro. Billy to drive." Bro. McEntyre was so thankful that he had obeyed God.

While driving the truck through Winchester, Tennessee, God began to lay a burden on Woody's heart to start a work in that town. The more often he drove through, the heavier the burden became until he, Jeannie, and their three children moved to Winchester and began a home mission work which is still thriving today. Thank God for people who obey!

Shortly thereafter, Bob and Billie Jean took the pastorate of a church in Tullahoma, Tennessee. It was a joyous time for Hazel, seeing her children involved in the work of God.

Billie Jean, Debbie, and Bob

Pictured to the right is Amber,
Hazel's great-granddaughter,
daughter of Cherryl. When Amber
was a little girl she ate some
chemicals that were poisonous.
When Hazel prayed, she was
touched, healed, and protected
by the Lord.

Now there were three outreaches
from her church. Being a woman pastor might have been a "thorn in the
flesh," but it surely had its rewards as well. She could not com-
plain. The world could never have given her the joy and fulfillment
that Jesus was giving her. He had promised to give her the desires
of her heart, and He was fulfilling that promise more and more as
time progressed.

The third location of the First United Pentecostal Church was
at 8190 Wilkinsville Road.

Chapter 8

HAZEL PURSUES HER DREAM

"And let us not be weary in well doing: for in due season we shall reap, if we faint not." (Galatians 6:9)

In September 1970, a large church building with a basement and Sunday school rooms located at 8190 Wilkinsville Road was purchased from the Church of Christ. (See picture at bottom on page 68.) This would ease the growing pains and was merely another step in the fulfillment of Hazel's Dream – she continued to talked about that **NEW church**.

Fifty people received the Holy Ghost in a very short time. The revival spirit continued. The first month the church purchased two Sunday School buses, and a bus ministry was later started.

One day the Lord gave Hazel a vision of a face. She did not know for sure why, but knew that one day she would see the woman in her vision. It was not long before Joan Cowan found her way to the one-God, Pentecostal Church at 8190 Wilkinsville Road. When she walked in, Hazel immediately recognized her as the woman in her vision. Within a week, Joan had received the Holy Ghost and was baptized in Jesus' name. Ten days later during a revival with Rev. Harold Smith, Linda, her daughter, received the Holy Ghost in the baptismal pool. Joan and Linda helped with the bus ministry as well as in other areas around the church. Joan had two sons, Edward and John, who about two years later received the Holy Ghost and were baptized during a youth service. Joan's husband had been transferred to Millington through the military, and when he retired from the navy, he moved his family to the Campbell County part of East Tennessee where Linda and Joan were instrumental in establishing a work for the Lord in LaFollette.

A radio broadcast ministry was started by Doug Wilbanks. He talked to the owner of the radio station who agreed to allow the broadcast to be aired at $10 for 30 minutes which was almost unheard of in that day!

A man from Memphis named Bro. Barney Vinney was washing his car and listening to the radio broadcast. He often told how he felt the love of God through the broadcast and felt the power of this love draw him to the church. He was baptized and received the Holy Ghost, which was a direct result of this outreach ministry.

Doug's wife, Gloria, was Ladies Auxiliary leader and Foreign Missions director. When she was seeking the Holy Ghost, she wanted to please the Lord so much that she gave her whole paycheck in the offering! Today Doug and Gloria Wilbanks attend Truth Tabernacle in Bakersfield, California.

Rev. R.W. (Wayne) and Linda Jones felt a call on their heart to go to Covington, Tennessee. They established a church that is a growing church today. God is faithful and will not forget the labor of love. Thank God for those who love God enough to sacrifice for His cause.

Hazel began to be even more excited about building that NEW church. The congregation also got a vision of that dream. The ladies kept making that peanut brittle and those chicken dinners. Many of the men sold the candy on their job. There was no doubt, Hazel and the church were moving to bigger and better things in God.

In April 1971, the former church building at Third and

Wilkinsville was sold, and the present building was paid in full. It took only seven months!

What a boost to Hazel's faith! She knew her dream was getting closer. She had already invisioned it in faith. She could almost see it in the natural now.

John and Lou Mattox, a military couple, came to the church in March, 1971. They received the Holy Ghost and were baptized in Jesus' name. Shortly thereafter, John was sent to Japan. It was a hard time for Lou and her little children with John gone. Hazel became a mother to her. She encouraged her, prayed with her, and always checked to see what she could do to help her.

One night when there was snow on the ground, Lou was getting out of the car at church and sprained her ankle. Hazel came out of the church, knelt down and prayed for her. God instantly healed her ankle!

God had sent another military couple from the church to Okinawa. They were Hank and Sue Whitsett. They started a church there. In 1973 Hazel won a trip overseas to visit a missionary family for giving the largest offering to Sheaves for Christ. She chose her "very own" missionary family - Hank, Sue, and their children. John Mattox heard about her being in Okinawa, so he flew from his base to join her and the church there. It was a wonderful reunion for all of them!

She often reminded her church, "God is just as big as you will let Him be. He is the same God that made the iron to float for Elijah and opened the Red Sea for the Israelites. If He could make

Hazel and Roy at Hank and Sue's Home in Okinawa.

Pictured (above) is Hazel with Sue and Hank in front of the Okinawa Church. Pictured (below) are Sue and her two children (left) and John, Hazel, and Roy (right).

the water stand up like walls yesterday, brother, He can do it today! If He could give them water out of the rock to drink, He can meet your needs, today. We don't want to ever limit God. That's why the Israelites were cut off, for unbelief. We don't want that to happen to us. He is the same yesterday, today, and forever. He is a God at hand and not afar off. Let's worship him!"

One Sunday night the church service was unusually "dry." Hazel stood up and said, "Satan does not have power to 'bind' this service unless God's people let him. Let's all raise our hands and praise God. He inhabits the praises of His people." The spirit of God began to mightily move among His people. God opened Hazel's "spiritual eyes" and she saw "hundreds of little legs" running out the front door of the church. God's people had bound the forces of satan by loosing the spirit of praise. (Matthew 16:19)

Dedication time was a very special time for Hazel. She would hold the newborn baby up for the congregation to see, tell its name, and say, "We have someone here who has never been to church in their life." And with a smile continue, " Isn't that a shame?" (She was not one to tell jokes in the pulpit, but she had her own sense of humor.) Dedication consisted of reading from I Samuel 1:27-28, *"For this child I prayed; and the Lord hath given me my petition, which I asked of him: Therefore also I have lent him to the Lord; as long as he liveth he shall be lent to the Lord. And he worshipped the Lord there."*

Then she explained to the parents what it meant to dedicate a child to God. She instructed them how to discipline with love and teach the child God's Word. She and the elders of the church would then laid their hands on the child and pray that God would bless it all the days of its life and use it to His glory. She always finished the dedication by giving the baby a BIG HUG!

Hazel was a friend to every age. There was not anyone who she could not relate to. Many of the children of the church received the Holy Ghost by the time they were five or six years old. One young boy wanted to be baptized when he received the Holy Ghost. His father asked Hazel, "Do you think he's old enough to

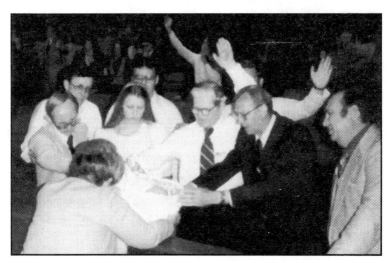

Baby dedication of Joshua Turner.

know what he is doing?" She replied, "No, but God knows what He is doing, giving him the Holy Ghost." She did not believe in baptizing infants, but Jesus did say, *"Suffer the little children to come unto me, and forbid them not: for of such is the king-dom of God."* (Mark 10:14) She baptized her grandchildren in the bathtub when they were old enough and desired it.

Debbie (the youngest granddaughter) developed rhuematic fever. Hazel went to pray for her. While she was there, she jumped rope with Debbie, even though she was fifty-five years old. Debbie has never forgotten that!

One Sunday morning, a lady brought her child

Hazel baptizing Sharon Ross.

in during worship service. The lady was crying out to God to heal her baby who had already turned blue. When Hazel prayed for the little girl, God healed her instantly.

Hazel really did had a soft spot for children. Once when Mark Turner had spent the weekend with his Dad, he came home feeling very badly because he had stayed up late. He did not feel like going to school but his Mom felt he just could not afford to miss any more days. She would not hear of his missing. He talked to Hazel and she went "to bat" for him. She persuaded Mom to let him stay home and it would be okay. You guessed it, It was!

Bro. Jeff Douglas came from Bethel Church in Memphis and organized the orchestra. There were many young people with instruments who wanted to play. This orchestra was such a blessing to the youth and to the church.

The Lord had blessed the church with soloists, duets, trios, and quartets, besides the choir and orchestra. Talent was never a problem. The anointing was always present.

A Kawai grand piano and a Hammond organ with Leslie speakers was purchased in addition to a good sound system.

Hazel and the church were getting ready for that **new** church building! It wouldn't be very long.

Dee Wells and Pam Wallace shared Hazel's dream. They served a lot of pancake breakfasts as well as serving "Sunday dinner" to the service men at the church. Everyone was so happy working for the Lord.

The youth department of the church decided to help buy a jeep for the missionary in Haiti. The Lord blessed the candy sales. Joan and Linda Cowan made and sold more than their share. Not only was the money sent for the jeep, $1200 was raised in two weeks for "Christmas for Christ," the home missions offering.

One day Linda Cowan and Vicky Turner were selling peanut brittle and had not sold very many bags. There was some kind of farm auction going on and Linda's dad suggested they go there. They were already discouraged but went anyway. They sold 100 bags in one hour!

Hazel had learned long ago that you could never outgive God, especially when it comes to the missionaries. She always believed that America had been especially blessed by God for sending missionaries to foreign countries. Those missionaries held a special place in her heart.

The church continued to grow as well as the outreach ministries. Two young couples went out on the evangelistic field full time, Mac and Celeste Bailey and Jeff and Judy Sanders.

Hazel and Roy took a trip to the Holy Land. It was such a blessing for them, since they had never gone before. God performed a miracle for her while she was there. One day, while they were touring, a sudden shower came. For some reason, everyone was given a rain hat except her. Her feelings were hurt until she realized that God allowed this for a testimony. Not ONE drop of water fell on her hair!

A sectional rally was being held at the church one Friday night when a young man who was a visitor asked Hazel if she had any experience casting out devils. "Yes," she replied. "Well, I have one," he said. Hazel thought he was just teasing, but when the service started and God began to bless, that spirit threw him. (Satan always likes to disrupt the worship of God and draw attention to himself.) Hazel was wise enough to take the young man to one of the Sunday school rooms. She and Sis. Durham cast the spirit out of him. *"In my name shall they cast out devils."* (Mark 16:17)

Julie Jenkins and several other young people from the church were returning home from youth camp with one of the deacons, Bro. Willingham, when a drunken driver rounded a curve and smashed in the driver's side of the car. Julie, who was in the back seat, was knocked unconcious. She was taken to Hazel's house. She was not home but her daughter, Billie Jean who was a registered nurse, examined her and found a broken shoulder. Her parents took her to the emergency room at St. Joseph Hospital where she was confirmed to have a clean break in her shoulder. She was given a brace and medication. On the way home, she went to sleep and did not remember Hazel coming by her house to pray for her, but her mother felt the power of God for instant healing during this prayer. When she awoke the next morning, she said, "I don't need this brace." Her parents took her back to the hospital where she was pronounced completely healed when x-rayed.

God never ceased to do the miraculous among His people. Richard Berford's (one of the deacons) daughter, Sheila stepped on a rusty spike nail in some old lumber. The nail punctured an artery in her foot. Everytime her heart beat, it sent a stream of blood into the air. When Richard picked her up and said, "In Jesus' name," the blood instantly stopped! It's so good that He is a God at hand and not afar off! His name is a strong tower!

The year, 1975, was a glorious year for Hazel and the church. Five acres of land was purchased at the corner of Shelby and Quito roads, which was the site where the original church burned.

Before it had burned, God had spoken through the gift of prophecy (I Corinthians 12:10) and said, "I have set my name in this place." Remembering this, Hazel was sure she was in God's perfect will purchasing this land.

The land was paid for in less than seven months! Thirty-five thousand dollars in seven months is not bad for a church of less than two hundred people! Hazel's faith really began to soar!

She really started talking about that **new** church then! A Red and Blue team was organized to support the building fund. Doris Berford, the ladies auxiliary leader, and the ladies worked hard on many projects. Everyone was excited about that new church. There were dinners, car washes, bake sales, and crafts. You name it, and the ladies worked at it to raise money.

Hazel expressed her appreciation to the church for how everyone was working. She said, "We are on our way, and I thank God! I know the devil doesn't want us to build it, but we are! I told the Lord that we are determined to build it!"

"I want to tell you people of God, if we unite together, there is no power that can stop us! If you want a memorial for God, **not for me**, you help build this church." She reminded the people how that when the first church burned there was no funds, but how God provided the down payment money by the time the papers were drawn up which took about 3 months. "That $2000 then was as much for the handful of people as $50,000 would be for us today." Her faith began to inspire the people even more.

New missionaries were supported by the church. The more money given to missions, the more that came into the treasury!

Hazel started a Bond program in October of 1977. The Lord really blessed this effort. The whole church was like a hive of working bees. Roy sold many of these bonds. $85,000 was gained through this effort, but there was $250,000 still to go.

Hazel pointed out to the church that God loves sacrifice. Jesus said, *"If any man will come after me, let him deny himself, and take up his cross, and follow me."* (Matthew 16:24) "This is a cross carrying way. We must carry a cross if we want to wear a crown. The early church counted it an honor to sacrifice for the Lord's sake and His gospel. Peter and John rejoice to be beaten and thrown in jail for Jesus' name! The Lord wants us to serve Him joyfully as we present our bodies a living sacrifice unto him. The joy of the Lord is our strength. With joy you shall draw water out of the wells of salvation. If we really believe God, we're going to have to act like it. God is faithful. He knows our need before we even ask, and it is His good pleasure to give us the kingdom. We don't have a thing to worry about or to hang our head over. Our Father is the King. He owns all the silver and the gold, the cattle on a thousand hills, the earth and the fullness thereof, and we are His children, the sheep of His pasture."

She continued, "He proved to Abraham that He would provide. We are Abraham's seed and heirs according to the promise. Like Caleb and Joshua, we are well able to take the land. Our God is on the move for us. He is leading us to victory. Praise His wonderful name! Faith is the substance of things hoped for, the evidence of things not seen (Hebrews 11:1) Our dream will be fulfilled. We shall build that new church for His great name's sake. Let's just start praising Him for it right now!"

But it wasn't all work! Hazel performed many weddings. You guessed it. She married couples in Jesus' name. *"And what-*

soever ye do in word or deed, do all in the name of the Lord Jesus, giving thanks to God and the Father by him." (Colossians 3:17)

Hazel praying a blessing over Denzil and Sheila Turner during their wedding.

Hazel with Cindi and John Johnson at their wedding.

Chapter 9

HAZEL'S DREAM
COMES TRUE

"Delight thyself also in the Lord; and he shall give thee the desires of thine heart." (Psalms 37:4)

Hazel had based her entire life on this scripture. The "Love of Christ" constrained her. She had counted it all joy to serve God, even when times were hard. "What an honor to serve the Lord of Lords and King of Kings!" she often said. "If we suffer with Him, we shall also reign with Him."

She would not allow anyone to apologize for calling her at late hours. "Oh, honey, that's my job. It's such a privilege to serve God and His people. Don't worry about it."

She wanted to be like her Lord who made of himself no reputation but took on the form of a servant. (Philippians 2:7) Her life was her example. She willingly gave of herself. Her love manifested itself in deeds to others.

Hazel and the church had envisioned a dream in faith, embraced it, and patiently waited for its fulfillment. Sure, she knew dreams could be costly. Nothing great comes without sacrifice, but she was prepared for that.

August 3, 1978 was the Big Day! Construction begun on that

"New Church" of her dreams. The design was the "Star of David."

She was so thankful that God was allowing her to build this church. David was one of her favorite bible characters, and she was a worshipper and prayed the Psalms of David many times.

His dream had been to build the temple, but God forbade it. She admired this man who was a man after God's own heart - one who praised and worshipped God in all circumstances.

Soon after construction had begun, many military families were shipped out. She encouraged the church. "God is faithful and His promises are "yea and amen." He has always provided for us in the past and will continue to do so. Let's not look at circumstances and get discouraged. We must not become weary in well doing. Our God will provide. He has never had to have a majority to win a battle, and He never will. Just trust Jesus! He never fails!"

The beams had been constructed when a long, cold, winter set in. The funds were so low that the work was progressing slowly. The beams and decking stood through six weeks of ice, snow, and freezing weather. The contractor greatly feared that they would warp. A man even came to one of the deacons and said, "Don't you know that snow is ruining that building?"

This would have been a time of great discouragement had not Hazel's faith been so strong. "We pay our tithes, God has promised to rebuke the devourer for our sake and pour us out a bless-

ing that there shall not be room enough to receive it. (Malachi 3:10-11) We must stand on His everlasting Word," she told the church. "We are being tried by fire. Remember, fire purifies. Jesus told us in Revelation 3:18, *'I counsel thee to buy of me gold tried by fire, that thou mayest be rich'*."

Hazel, who had always taken a modest salary, let everything possible go into the building fund. Roy supported her and it was their desire to lay up treasures in heaven and not on this earth. (However, the missionaries were not neglected.)

A loan of $72,000 was negotiated on the church at 8190 Wilkinsville and work began to pick up.

Finally in November, several church families borrowed money (the church later paid it back). They gave of their finances, and they helped with the finishing work on the inside of the building.

Then came the long awaited day – on December 24, 1979, the first service was conducted in this new church. The presence of the Lord flooded the sanctuary as Nancy Childress sang, "How Great Thou Art." The congregation stood and with raised hands

The present church at Shelby and Quito roads – a monument built unto the Lord.

worshipped the One who had made this dream possible.

Hazel's heart just overflowed as she brought the message that Sunday morning. God had been glorified; even the contractor called it a "Miracle Church."

At the dedication service, she recalled when she went to pray for little Dale Turner, who was sick. She was very sick herself at the time. When she mentioned this to Dale's mother, his other brother (Denzil) and sister (Vicky), laid their small hands on her and prayed for her. They had the faith of God in their hearts. She told how God instantly healed her, because of the faith of a child!

She had been told, "When you get in that fancy church with padded pews and stained glass windows, you won't have the kind of services that you have been having." Of course, she did not believe this. Her God deserved the very best!

She knew that the truth and holiness would be preached in this place. It would be a soul saving station. She loved souls more than anything in the world – they were her number one priority!

"I am trying to be an example to you in prayer, fasting, and witnessing for God," she said. "This is something that we must do. God asks us to present our bodies a living sacrifice. We must do it for it is our reasonable service. There are people dying and going to hell. Jesus said, 'Ye have not chosen me, but I have chosen you, and ordained you, that ye should go and bring forth fruit, and that your fruit should remain; that whatsoever ye shall ask of the Father in my name, he may give it you.' We must bear fruit. Jesus said, 'Abide in me and I in you. As the branch cannot bear fruit of itself except it abide in the vine; no more can ye except ye abide in me. If a man abide not in me, he is cast forth as a branch, and is withered and men do gather them and cast them into the fire and they are burned. If ye abide in me and my words abide in you, ye shall ask what you will and it shall be done unto you. Herein is my father glorified that ye bear much fruit. So shall ye be my disciples' (John 15:4-8)."

Truly, she had been an example. She would never ask the church to do something that she would not do herself. In broken manner, she would often say, "I love you all even more that I love myself. I want you to be saved more than anything in this world. We must bear fruit. Jesus saved us to be soul winners. We must be about the Father's business for night cometh when no man can work." God had given her a harvest of souls for her labor. Her own three lovely granddaughters were working for the Lord.

Hazel left a tremendous heritage to her granddaughters. From left to right are Debbie, Sheila, and Cherryl.

Doug Wilbanks had felt this love for souls the very first time he came to church. It captivated him. He had never felt anything like it before. There was such a bond with God's people. It was stronger than the ties you feel with your biological family. Hazel taught and practiced the same love that Jesus meant when He said, "By this shall all men know that ye are my disciples, if ye have love one to another." (John 13:35)

Hazel got a call from Pastor Barnette, who wanted to buy the building at 8190 Wilkinsville Rd. She had prayed that the building would be sold to someone who preached the truth. She witnessed to him about one God and Jesus' name baptism. (God later revealed it to him, and Pastor Travis Sheppard baptized him; he received the Holy Ghost and preaches the truth in that building.)

Pastor Barnette purchased the church at 8190 Wilkinsville. The amount would finish paying off the loan that was negotiated to finish the new church. This transaction turned out to be a blessing for all involved. It lifted the financial load off the church.

Chapter 10

HAZEL DREAMS AGAIN

"Now unto him that is able to do exceedingly abundantly above all that we ask or think, according to the power that worketh in us." (Ephesians 3:20)

Roy and Hazel cutting their Golden Anniversary wedding cake.

In 1980, Roy and Hazel celebrated their golden wedding anniversary.

Hazel began to dream again! This time it was for a Christian school. She felt there was a great need for this school. Even though she had only an eighth grade formal education, she pioneered a Christian Day School in the church fellowship hall. She went to Leesville, Texas and took the A.C.E. training (Accelerated Christian Education). She passed with a 90% average. God was flooding her life with His blessings!

Bro. Willingham made a little red school house to collect funds for the proposed new school building.

She and the church had a good financial report with local businesses. A building supply company told her she could purchase anything she wanted. That was all she needed to hear. In 1982 a new school building was built and completly paid for!

God was true to His promises. Hazel and the church had unselfishly supported missionaries, and God had richly blessed for this effort. The church was now supporting 80. This amounted to $2,000 a month. The vestibule was covered with pictures of these missionaries.

Also in 1982, the international award was presented to her for the fastest growing Sunday School in North America in the United Pentecostal Church International organization (percentage wise). It was one of many!

For years, Hazel had desired more education. In 1983, she graduated from Pioneer Pentecostal College with a ABS Degree. She recieved the Pioneer Pentecostal College Award for soul winning. She had baptized about 2,000 souls in Jesus' name!

Hazel Simpson on "Graduation Day" from Pioneer Pentecostal College. Hazel is in the last row, first person on the left. What a joyous occasion that was for her!

She began to dream again! This time it was a gym for the children of the school to have a place to play when it was cold or raining. It could also be used by the church for singings, fellowship dinners, and a place for the young military men who wanted to spend Sunday afternoon away from the base. She took pledges to build the gym. Participation was great.

She reflected back on the goodness of God. He had told her in 1978, that the church would be paid for in five years. Not only had the church been paid for, but she had built a new school and it was paid for too. She rejoiced in the Lord! The following article, which appeared in The Defender, sums it all up.

We Went Through The Fire . . .

By Pat Warren as told to Dee Wells

Last Sunday morning our pastor stood up before the congregation and stated that we had paid off our new church. Needless to say this really brought back many memories to me.

Not long after I received the Holy Ghost in November 1963, I can remember my pastor was talking about building a new church. As the years went by, it looked like she would not see her dream come true. In 1970, we purchased the old Church of Christ building on Wilkinsville Road, but she still talked about building a **new** church.

Finally, in June 1975, we learned that there was five acres of land for sale at the corner of Quito and Shelby Road. This just happened to be the site of our very first mission church which began in the Spring of 1958 and later burned. Prior to the burning, God had spoken through the gift of prophecy (I Corinthians 12:10) and said, "I have set my name in this place." Remembering the words of the Lord, we were confident that it was God's will to purchase this property. Even though we were a small church of less than 200, we had this property paid for in seven months. Not a small amount either!

Plans were drawn up for our new church.

I can remember that whenever we talked about building a new church, it seemed that money would start coming in from everywhere, and then when we would stop talking about building one, the money would really drop off. We felt the Lord wanted us to step out on faith and start building a new church. So, after the land was paid for, we began the process of obtaining the backing to build this church. Trying every financial institution that we could think of and having no success whatsoever, we finally started a bond program in October 1977. I might add that we were running 200 in Sunday School then and felt that a growth definitely was in progress and we could pay the bonds off when we had to. The Lord was so good, too, and allowed us to sell $85,000 in bonds. Of course, this was still short of the $250,000 that we needed.

On August 3, 1978, we stepped out on faith and started the church and at that time we had a little over $100,000 in our treasury. **Hebrews 11:1 states,** *"Now faith is the substance of things hoped for, the evidence of things not seen."* Right after we started to build our church, many of our Navy families were shipped out. From that day on, and I guess until last Sunday, I really got an opportunity to understand what that scripture meant.

First of all, we found out right away that we were very short of money. Work was almost completely stopped right in the middle of winter 1978, a year before completion. The beams were in the ceiling but the shingles were not on. I can remember going to the church and seeing it open and snow on the paper that was covering the beams, and everyone telling me that when it melted it would seep through and stain the ceiling and the beams. IT DIDN'T! I can remember praying and praying about the money situation, and so many of the other problems that we encountered during the building of this church. The Lord told me that work would not stop on this church. **IT NEVER DID. It slowed down, but it never stopped.** During this time a scripture was given to me. It was Psalms 66:10-12: *"For thou, O God, hast proved us: thou has tried us, as silver is tried. Thou broughtest us into the net; thou laidst affliction upon our loins. Thou hast caused men to ride over our heads; we went through fire and through water: but thou broughtest us out into a wealthy place."*

I guess we did every thing that we could to raise money. I do not think in the entire history of this ministry, neither before nor since, we have had so many contests. I know it was pleasing to the Lord to see all of His people working like we did. I think for awhile, after the **crunch** was over, I had a hard time looking peanut brittle in the face. But God blessed our peanut brittle. I could not tell you how many bags we sold, a few thousand I guess. I know we all got depressed and discouraged during this time of our trial by fire. I still can remember people asking me if I thought this church would ever be built. The only answer that I had was that we as a church had always paid our tithes, and God was bound by His word. We had also been faithful to support many missionaries to whom we had pledged support prior to the building program.

Finally, in September 1979, we were able to negotiate a loan on the building on Wilkinsville Road. We borrowed $72,000, but that was still not enough to complete the church. It did help speed up the process, however. In November 1979, several families borrowed money to help us finally finish the church. We paid them back at a later date.

We paid a man $4,000 to pave a parking lot. He did little. All he did was dump some gravel and run off with the money. The Lord had given the following scriptures in November.

Isaiah 41:10-13, *"Fear thou not; for I am with thee: be not dismayed; for I am thy God: I will strengthen thee; yea, I will help thee; Behold, all they that were incensed against thee shall be ashamed and confounded: they shall be as nothing; and they that strive with thee shall perish. Thou shall seek them, and shall not find them, even them that contended with thee: they that war against thee shall be as nothing and as a thing of naught. For I the Lord thy God will hold thy right hand, saying unto thee, fear not; I will help thee."*

On the Sunday before Christmas 1979, we had our first service in our new church. At that time we still had $50,000 in outstanding debts, and a man threatening to take our windows out again after he had put them in because we could not pay him.

We are not wealthy, but when we had been tried like He said in Psalms 66:10-13, the blessings of God started on our church, and the rest is history.

In recapping, it really is impressive. June 1975, we bought the land, in 1976 we paid for the land, in 1977 the bond program, 1978 we started the church, in 1979 we moved in the church, in 1980 we paved the parking lot, in 1982 we built our school. Then in December 1983 and it was all paid for.

We are definitely not a rich people except in the Lord. *(But God has chosen the poor of this world but rich in faith . . .)* **and of course, He owns all the silver and all the gold - and the NEARLY ONE-HALF MILLION DOLLARS THAT PAID THIS ALL OFF!**

God . . Brought Us Out Into A Wealthy Place.

Pictured HERE is the NEW CHURCH at Quito and Shelby roads. God has truly put His name and blessing on this place.

These pictures show views of the sanctuary that was built to house the presence of God, a place where worship could be sent up as a sweet savour unto the Lord. Jeannie Tenney is blessing the church with her beautiful singing (above). Tommy Tenney (seated in center) preached that service. The Paul Durham Group is pictured below entertaining the Spirit of God. God has a beautiful place to meet with His saints.

Chapter 11

GOD BLESSES HAZEL'S DREAM CHURCH

God continued to bless the church. It was common to hear testimonies like this one, written by Bro. Douglas Blevins.

The faith and love for the truth that I have today was instilled in me by Sis. Simpson's preaching and ministry.

When I was about 14 years old, I did something so bad that even today, I don't want to tell. There was no way that anyone knew about it.

Sis. Simpson came up to me at church and said, "Dougie, the Lord showed me . . . (and she proceeded to tell me what I had done). You need to repent." I thought I would really get in trouble with my Mom and Dad, but she never told them. I repented, but I never forgot that. She had the true spirit of discernment in her life.

When I was about 12 years old, a great miracle happened. I was playing in our front yard with a spindle of wire attached to a kite, flying it. I had my thumbs in the spool of wire and was guiding it with my "pointer finger." When the wind shifted, the kite hit the main electrical high line. A bolt of fire hit me and bounced me about three feet off the ground. Later we found out that the electricity went off about two and one-half miles down the road! I ran in the house scream-ing. I was in shock and didn't know what hit me. My uncle, Roy Ross, came running down the hill. He lived next door and had seen it happen. (Roy is a deacon in Millington U.P.C. Church, today.) He told my Mom what he saw.

She called Sis. Simpson and in a short time about 25 people gathered at our house, all agreeing in fer-vent prayer. My Mom took my shoes off. My big toes looked like raw hamburger; my thumbs were melted. There was the smell of burned flesh. I was hurting really bad until everyone prayed for me.

We had church service the next night. I could hardly move. Mom didn't think I was well enough to go, but I wanted to go. My cousin carried me. I couldn't walk. Everyone prayed for me again.

I had to miss school and someone sent the welfare department to our house. The lady who came was real hateful. She told my Mom and Dad to take me to the doctor or the department would MAKE them.

I had such great faith, even though I was young. I had seen so many people in our church healed and was taught such faith that I spoke up and told the lady, "I don't want to go to the doctor because I am trusting in God."

My parents believed God, but they took me to the doctor. The doctor said, "There isn't anything I can do. Your son should be dead. What you see is only the outside - he should be cooked on the inside!"

He gave them some ointment to put on my toes. Later the man from the light company told us that he had seen men burned black and killed with the voltage that went through me. That HE knew it was a miracle!

Today, I have the edge of both thumbs still missing. I believe God left that as a reminder to me of what He did for me.

(Doug Blevins and his wife are youth leaders of Praise Tabernacle in Munford, Tennessee.)

Sylvia Warren was at Hazel's house one day. They were going to pray for the sick. She had been in the church about three months. Hazel was fixing Roy's lunch before they left. She forgot that she had already salted the beans. When she went to put more salt in, she was in a hurry and poured too much in. She asked Sylvia to taste them. Sylvia, who liked her food salty, found the beans so salty she could hardly stand them. Hazel said, "That's alright, we are going to pray and the Lord won't let them taste salty."

After they prayed, Sylvia tasted the beans again. They were bland! She was amazed. In the years since, she has seen God heal cancer and all sorts of things but nothing has amazed her more than this.

Joyce Laird had surgery for ovarian cancer. She had one ovary removed and part of the other one. It was her heart's desire to be a joyful mother of children. The doctor said this was impossible. Hazel prayed for her and God healed her. The Lord gave her the following scripture.

"Sing, Oh, barren that didst not travail with child: for more are the children of the desolate than of the married wife, saith the Lord. Enlarge the place of thy tent, and let them stretch forth the curtains of thine habitations: spare not, lengthen thy cords and strengthen thy stakes. For thou shalt break forth on the right hand and on the left..."

Her first child was a girl named Deborah. Then God blessed her with twin girls, Rachel and Rebecca. Next came a son, Randy. Now she is a grandma!

God is faithful who promised.

One night, when Hazel was suffering excruicating pain from kidney stones, the Lord spoke to her and told her to have Roy pray for her. She got the bottle of oil and asked Roy to pray. She was instandly healed!

God had blessed the church with a Spanish ministry under the direction of Bro. Don De La Rosa. He held service every Thursday night with about 20-30 Spanish-speaking people.

Then there was the Jetway Military ministry under the direction of Freddie Turner. The youth of the church stood at the Jetway Shopping center near the main gate of the Naval Base. They invited young service men and women to church. A van picked them up at the main gate fifteen minutes before each church service. Many souls were added to the church through this ministry.

Wade Price and Matthew Bellonis, two young servicemen reached through the Jetway Military ministry.

Once when the youth had been witnessing there, they met a devil worshipper. They brought him to Hazel's house. She witnessed to him, prayed for him, and God delivered him. He confessed to her, "I had polio when I was a child. A preacher prayed for me, and I was healed. I know God is real."

Two young ministers of the church, Bro. Mike Edmaiston and Bro. Dale Rushing, worked in the nursing home ministry. They held services at many rest homes.

The outreach director was praying with them before they went to their services when she saw a vision. A beacon light was shining from the church. Its beams reached afar.

Hazel helped with these services, too. She prayed for a lady who was visiting her mother at the Care Inn Rest Home. This lady had lost hearing in one ear. God healed her instantly. When the lady was returning home on an airplane, she met one of Hazel's converts who was a pastor's wife, and told her of the healing. Judy, who lived in Philadelphia, called home and told her mother. This Light HAD spread AFAR! God always confirms His Word.

Hazel attended these rest home services on Sunday afternoon and her own two services at the church.

God had also blessed the church with a deaf ministry. Barbara Means interpreted for the deaf during services. She was assisted by Marie Witte. A couple came into the church who had a deaf son. Lewis gained most most of his knowledge of the Bible because this ministry was started. His mother, Sis. Laurie Klinedenst, was director of the deaf ministry in the church.

The church had a youth ministry as well as an adult choir and a youth choir. The young ministers preached on Saturday night and served the church in various ways.

Two other outreaches had been established from the church. Bro. and Sis. McEntrye had started a church in Somerville, Tennessee, and Bro. Alan Wilson had gone to pastor in Louisiana.

The church had an outreach paper, "The Defender." It was circulated in many states and overseas. Mike and Patti Edmaiston were editors until they went on the evangelistic field. Joe and Cindy Culp replaced them. Bro. James Basham wrote regularly for the paper. This was a testimony in itself because Bro. Basham wrote this from the Veterans Hospital. He was partially paralyzed and in a wheelchair. A newsletter was sent each month to the servicemen after they were transferred from Millington to encourage them. Some of them held Bible studies on their ships.

There was also a prison ministry. Once after Bro. Mac Bailey had preached at Ft. Pillow Prison, he received a letter from an inmate. The inmate told Bro. Bailey that when he was preaching his footsteps had formed a cross, and he wanted to know more about the plan of salvation.

Testimonies like these continued:

Bro. Tommy Warren, a deacon in the Millington church today, told this testimony.

> I was driving a tanker truck hauling gas for Gulf Oil Company. I was going to Blyville, Arkansas on I-55. The Lord spoke to me and said, "Pull Over." I hesitated and He spoke again. The third time he said, "PULL OVER!" I did. When I checked my truck over, I found that the frame was broken in two. If I would not have stopped, all the weight of the tanker would have run over the top of the cab and not only crushed it, but it would have exploded!
>
> My truck had to be towed in for repairs. The men where I worked were amazed. They asked me, "How did you know to pull over?" I told them that God had told me to pull over!

Bro. Larry Ridley, who still attends the Millingon church today, has this wonderful testimony.

> "My son and myself were changing out the stove pipe in my fireplace. We had a 25-foot chimney. We had taken out the old triple wall pipe, but when I looked up I saw some pipe still stuck at the top. I shoved my son out of the way, and the pipe fell and hit me on the side of my back before I could get out. I couldn't move. My wife called her sister who called Sis. Simpson. It took about 25 minutes or more before Sis. Simpson, Sis. Durham, and her sister and son, arrived to pray for me. I still could not move. I was laying where it fell on me.
>
> After they prayed, the Lord mightily touched me. I still have the scar from that triple wall pipe on my back today. I know prayer and great faith kept me from being paralyzed.
>
> Sis. Simpson always taught us to obey the voice of

God. And no matter where we were or what we were
doing if the Lord moved on us to pray, do it RIGHT
THEN!

At the same time I had the accident, Sis. Means,
my sister-in-law, and her family were eating. The Lord
moved on them to pray, that something was wrong.
They left their food sitting on the table and all prayed.
As they were praying, my wife, Linda, called them to
tell them what had happened to me. They were thankful that they had obeyed God's voice.

Sis. Agnes English met Wade Price at the store where she
worked. Wade was a young sailor who attended Hazel's church.
He was always talking about her and wanted Agnes to go with
him to visit her. Agnes did not want to go without being invited, so
she sat in the car while Wade went inside. In just a little while,
Hazel came out to the car and talked with her. While Hazel was
standing there talking, she put her hand on Agnes' side and prayed
for her. Agnes was amazed since she had not told Hazel that she
had a pulled muscle which had been hurting her for five years.
Doctor's had not helped it. Jesus knew where it was and healed
her! She still attends the Millington church today!

Nancy Childress found employment as the church's nursery
attendant. She heard the gospel and wanted to attend church
services instead. We lost a nursery attendant but gained a sister. She was baptized and recieved the Holy Ghost. She has been
a great blessing in our church with her singing. Today, she is a
faithful worker in the prison ministry of the church. Her son, daughter, and son-in-law are also faithful workers in the church today.

Dale Turner had 18 viral warts on his hands. His sister, Vicky,
"stood in for him" and was prayed for that the warts would leave
her brother's hands. The warts turned black and fell off.

Vicky's sister, Cindy, had teeth that were growing crooked,
and the family could not afford braces. So, Vicky prayed for her
sister. Cindy's teeth are beautiful today. They are "testimony teeth."
Prayer changes things.

Sis. Durham had gall stones. The Lord showed Hazel these stones in a vision, and she saw that she held her hand on the place where the stones were until they all disappeared. It happened just as she had seen it.

Hazel often reminded the church of two incidents God did for her through the gift of working of miracles. She had been busy working for the Lord and had forgotten to get gas. When she was a long distance from the service-station, she noticed her gas hand was on empty. She told the people who were in her car that they all must pray. They prayed and her car ran out of gas a few feet from the gas pumps.

On another occasion, she was driving from Memphis, when a man pulled along side her and said, "Lady your tire is flat." She told Sis. Durham, "We need to pray because I don't know how to change a flat tire. I don't want to be late for church." She just kept on driving. When she reached the church, her tire was full of air! Those riding with her were amazed.

Sis. Bessie Atkins was a lady Hazel met while inviting people to church. Her husband had just left her and she was lonely. She attended church that night. She was shy at first, but the Lord gave her boldness to go to the altar and pray. She was filled with the Holy Ghost and helped Hazel in the work of the Lord for several years before she moved away. After 30 years, God put her and her husband back together again. He had heart problems and went up for prayer. The Lord healed him and he was baptized in Jesus name. They had four happy years together before the Lord called him home. (This was Doug Wilbanks' Mom and Dad.)

Sis. Faye Smith testified that when her daughter, Cindi, was a baby, she had two teeth grow behind her two front teeth. She was young and scared, so she told Aunt Hazel about this. She said, "We are going to pray and believe God. Don't even look at her mouth, just believe God." So she obeyed. One day while she was playing with Cindi, she laughed real big, and Faye noticed that those teeth were gone!

When Bro. and Sis. Smith were on the evangelistic field, a cat scratched their other daughter, Sonia; her leg became infected and she contacted erysipelas. Her temperature was very high. Faye called Aunt Hazel, and they agreed that God would heal Sonia. Though Sonia was only two, she said "Mommy, where did the man go that had the scar in his hand?" Faye later tesified that she said, "Oh, Lord, please don't take her," thinking that the Lord was going to take Sonia. But immediately her temperature broke, and she was healed.

Faye Smith

On another occasion, when Cindi was four years old, she became very ill and was running a very high temperture.When we prayed, it would get better, but it would not go away. (The Lord had showed Aunt Hazel that she had polio, but she did not tell Faye.) Her hubsand got Cindi a talking doll, but she was too sick to play with it. One day, Cindi went into a convulsion. Faye called Aunt Hazel. She told Faye, "Faye, I feel the worst is yet to come. God tested Abraham's love by asking him to offer his son. You are called to do a work for God, and you must be strong. Faye took her baby in her arms and held her tightly. Then she did the hardest thing she ever did in her life. She said, "Lord, she's in your hands. If you want her, take her; just don't

Cindi Smith

let her suffer." She laid her on the bed and fell on her face before God and prayed. In just a little while, she heard the doll talking. She thought someone had come into the room. She looked up and saw her baby completely well playing with that doll. She had not even been able to walk. God had healed her instantly. She thanked God for grace to pass that hard test.

Once when they were on their way to preach a revival in Vardaman, Mississippi, they were pulling a camper trailer when they ran out of gas just a short distance from a service station. They were able to get the car off the road, but they couldn't get the trailer off. Faye stayed there while her hubsand went to the nearby gas station. A lady pulled up and said, "Get off the road." She blocked the view of an oncoming car which hit Faye and knocked her several feet into the air. She went in and out of consciousness. When the ambulance arrived, she asked to be taken to the church at Vardaman. The driver did not want to, so she decided to go to a sister's house. He liked that better. The church prayed for her. The next day, a state trooper came to check on

The Harold and Faye Smith Family

her. He was suprised that she was doing so well. He could not believe that she was the one involved in the accident. However, she still could not move her leg. God sent Bro. and Sis. Hill from Bruce, Mississippi to pray for her. When they prayed, God healed her leg. She started running and praising God!

When they were preaching another revival Bubba, their son, badly burned his leg on a heater. They began to pray. The pastor and his wife came over. It made her sick and she walked away. They called Aunt Hazel; she prayed and he went to sleep. That pastor told his church that they trusted God for healing and called a prayer meeting that night for Bubba. They prayed and God completely healed him. Aunt Hazel said that God had allowed this to happen to show His power to these people.

When they were pastoring a small church and were suffering financilly, Aunt Hazel told them that God would make a way when there seemeth no way. They were struggling to pay their truck note. They continued to pray and trust God. A man whose wife attended their church came one Sunday morning and asked to talk to them privately. They went into the kitchen and he handed them a check. They thanked him polietly and didn't even look at the check. When they looked at it , they saw it was for $3,500.

Sandra Ross was about 10 years old and had warts on the back of her ankle. It hurt to wear shoes, and she had to keep bandaids on them. Hazel prayed for her, but they did not go away.

Sandra's mom heard Sis. Faye Smith testify how two teeth had been growing behind the front teeth of Cindi and how Hazel told her after she had prayed not to even look at it again – just start praising God. And one day when the baby laughed, she noticed that the teeth were gone!

So, Sandra's mother she said she should do the same about the warts. One day Sandra came running to her and said, "Look! My warts are gone."

Bro. Roy Ross had ulcers since he was a teenager. Hazel prayed for him. She told him, "The Lord has healed your ulcers!" He never had anymore problem. Years later he had to have some tests done at the hospital. When the doctor looked at the x-rays, he said, "I can see a scar where you had an ulcer at one time."

Hazel rejoiced in the Lord for the wonderful testimonies that God had given His children. She felt like David when he said, "Oh give thanks unto the Lord; call upon His name, make **His deeds known among the people**. Sing unto Him, sing Psalms unto Him: **Talk of all His wondrous works**. Glory ye in His holy name: let the heart of them rejoice that seek the Lord. Seek the Lord, and His strength; seek His face evermore. Remember His marvelous works that he hath done: His wonders and the judgments of His mouth." She always encouraged the saints to testify, "You are made overcomers by the word of your testimonies and the blood of the Lamb. When you testify, don't tell a thing the devil's done. Jesus deserves all the honor and glory. He alone is worthy!"

God had fulfilled so many of her dreams in the last few years; dreams that went back to her childhood. Like David, she wanted to give Him glory for His mighty acts.

She often quoted one of her favorite passages of scripture: *"Behold, what manner of love the father hath bestowed upon us, that we should be called the sons of God: therefore the world knowest us not, because it knew Him not. Beloved, now are we the sons of God, and it doth not yet appear what we shall be: but we know that, when He shall appear, we shall be like Him; for we shall see Him as He is. And every man that hath this hope in Him purifieth himself, even as He is pure."* (I John 3:1-3)

She often told the church, "We must love one another. That's how Jesus said all men would know his disciples. We should never speak evil of one another. God's word says speak evil of no man. What we do to the least of God's children, we do to Him. We should be willing to lay down our life for the brethren. Jesus was our perfect example. Remember the love of God is shed abroad in our hearts by the Holy Ghost. (Romans 5:5) He gives the Holy Ghost to them that obey Him. (Acts 5:32) We must be obedient if we want to hear Jesus say <u>well done</u>. For if ye live after the flesh ye shall die: but if ye through the Spirit do mortify the deeds of the body, ye shall live. For as many as are led by the Spirit of God, they are the sons of God. (Romans 8:13-14) Paul went on to say that the sufferings of this present world are not even worthy to be compared with the glory that shall be revealed in us. If we suffer with him, we shall also reign with him. We must be longsuffering with others for Jesus was longsuffering with us. Like the Apostle Paul, I have not shunned to declare unto you all the counsel of God."

"Study God's word, hide it away in your heart like David," she admonished, "so you won't sin against it. Remember you will be judged by it on judgment day. (Revelation 20:12) You must know the truth before you can love it. And, don't forget there is just ONE LORD, ONE FAITH, ONE BAPTISM." (Ephesians 4:5) She taught that the one baptism is made up of two parts - water and spirit, and that we see a type of this when the Israelites were baptized by Moses in the cloud (Spirit) and in the sea (water). (I Corinthians 10:2) That's what Jesus meant when He told Nicodemus, *"Verily, Verily, I say unto thee, except a man be born of water and of the Spirit, he cannot enter the kingdom of God."* (St. John 3:5)

She continued, "Some say baptism is not essential, but Jesus said, *'He that believeth and is baptized shall be saved, but he that believeth not shall be damned.'* (Mark 16:16) For those who ask about the thief on the cross. He died between the law and grace (Luke 16:16, John 7:39). Paul told the Philippian jailer to believe on the Lord Jesus Christ and he would be saved and so would his household, yet he took them out and baptized them at midnight. (Acts 16:31-34) He said in Galatians 3:27, *"For as many of you as have been baptized into Christ have put on Christ."* That means we wear His precious name. Revelation 22:4 says, *"His name shall be in their foreheads."* His bride will wear His name. Most people aren't aware that everyone was baptized (immersed) in Jesus Name until 325AD when at the Council of Nicea, both the mode and formula were changed to sprinkling and infant baptism was instituted." (References: *The*

Encyclopaedia Britannica, Volume 3, pages 365 and 368, 1910 edition. *A Dictionary of the Bible* by James Hastings, Volume 1, page 241, 1906 edition.)

Paul also said in Galations 1:8, *"But though we, or an angel from Heaven, preach any other gospel unto you than that which we have preached unto you, let him be accursed."* Let's see what gospel Paul preached.

"Acts 19:1-7, *'And it came to pass, that, while Apollos was at Corinth, Paul having passed through the upper coasts came to Ephesus: and finding certain disciples, He said unto them, Have ye received the Holy Ghost since ye believed? And they said unto him, We have not so much as heard if there be any Holy Ghost. And he said unto them, Unto what then were ye baptized? And they said, Unto John's baptism. Then said Paul, John verily baptized with the baptism of repentance, saying unto the people, that they shoud believe on him which should come after him that is, on Christ Jesus. When they heard this, they were* **baptized** *in the* **name of the Lord Jesus**. *And when Paul had laid his hands upon them, the* **Holy Ghost** *came upon them; and they* **spake with tongues**, *and* **prophesied**. *And all the men were about twelve'."*

This 'Jesus' name gospel was what Paul preached and he told us not to believe **even an angel** if he came preaching **another gospel**. When Jesus gave Peter the keys to the kingdom, he preached the very same message. "Repent and be baptized **everyone** in the **name of Jesus Christ for the remission of sins**, and ye shall recieve the gift of the Holy Ghost." (Acts 2:38) In Acts the Second chapter, the Apostle Peter opened the door of the kingdom to the Jews here. He opened the doors to the Samaritans (or a mixed breed of people) in Acts 8:16-17, and finally to the first Gentiles in Acts 10:46-48. There is only one Gospel for all races of men.

All people had to come through that same door into the kingdom. The disciples **obeyed Jesus' command in Matthew 28:19** when they all baptized in Jesus' name. They understood what He meant when He said to baptize in the name of the Father, and of the Son, and of the Holy Ghost. (Matthew was present in Acts 2:38 when Peter said, *repent and be baptized every one of you in the name of Jesus Christ for the remission of sins . . .*) Jesus said, "I am the door." He also said in St. John 14:6-9, *"I am the way, the truth, and the life: no man cometh to the Father, but by me. If ye had known me, ye should have known my Father also: and from henceforth you know him, and have seen him. Philip saith unto him, Lord, shew us the Father, and it sufficeth us. Jesus saith unto him, Have I been so long time with you, and yet has thou not known me, Philip? he that hath seen me hath seen the Father; and how sayest thou then, shew us the Father."* Jesus said, *"I and my Father are one."* (John 10:30) This is the Gospel of the Kingdom.

"And this *gospel of the kingdom* shall be preached in all the world for a witness unto all nations, and *then the end shall come.*" (Matthew 24:14) *"For the kingdom of God is not meat and drink; but righteousness, and peace, and joy in the Holy Ghost."* (Romans 14:17).

God's people are so fortunate to know this glorious truth. The prophets and the angels desired to look into it but were not permitted to. We should never take it for granted but be willing to give our lives for it if necessary. What a thrill to know that Jesus Christ is the Mighty God, the Everlasting Father, and the Prince of Peace. The Bible says He came to his own and they received Him not. His nation just couldn't understand. They thought he was a man making himself God. The truth was that God, the invisible spirit (John 4:24), made Himself man so he could shed blood for our sins. Jesus is the image of the invisible God. (Colossians 1:15) A spirit can't shed blood and without the shedding of blood there is no remission of sins. (Hebrews 9:22)

The prophet foresaw the day when Jehovah would robe himself in flesh to become our salvation. Isaiah 12:1-2, *"In that day thou shalt say . . . the Lord Jehovah is my strength and song. He also is become my salvation."* "Neither is there salvation in any other; for there is none other name under heaven given among men, whereby we must be saved." (Acts 4:12)

Chapter 12

HAZEL'S DREAM LIVES ON

*"The Memory of the just is
blessed . . ."* (Proverbs 10:7)

*"That I may know Him, and the power of His resurrection,
and the fellowship of His sufferings, **being made conformable unto His death.** "* (Philippians 3:10)

Hazel began to realize that there was an affliction in her body.
She shared this privately with Sis. Durham. She had always taught
her people that even though they had seen God do the miraculous, there would still come a time when it would not be God's will
to heal . . . that we all must die unless Jesus returns first. She did
not tell the church about her affliction at that time but continued to
seek God's will.

Her condition grew steadily worse. God gave her a vision. In
this vision, she saw the demons having a meeting devising every
scheme they could to destroy the church. She asked the secretary
to make a list of all the men in the church who paid tithes. She
charged these men to "stand in the gap and make up the hedge"
by praying for the church. "Satan has plans to destroy this church.
We must stand strong!" she said.

The elders started a fasting and prayer chain, which strengthened them, but her condition did not improve. However, she continued to praise and worship her God.

A man of God came to pray for her. While he was praying, he saw two flights which would soon take place. He wanted to speak faith and believe that Hazel would be healed and see revival, but God had other plans.

God later spoke through the gifts of tongues and intrepretation (I Corinthians 12:10) and said, "I have seen your faith. It is even as the faith of Abraham and it has come up as a memorial before me. You have paved the way for others to follow."

When asked how she liked the new church sound system, she replied, "I like it but I won't need one in New Jerusalem where I'm going."

Then, in the last few days of her life, God spoke again, "My dear child I desire to bring you home with me."

"Precious in the sight of the Lord is the death of his saints." (Psalm 116:15)

September 30, 1984, Hazel took that heavenly flight. About 600 people crowded into the church for her HOMEGOING SERVICE! The choir sang, "I'll have a New Life." They shouted and worshipped as they sang. She would have loved that! Bro. Don Johnson sang, "We're not in the Valley." Her beloved "Millington Quartet" sang, "Just Wait Until You See My Brand New Home." Bro. Greer and Bro.Benson commended her stewardship. The Youth Choir sang, "Beulah Land," as the presence of the Lord permeated the sanctuary.

Roy was grief stricken. "I've lost my best friend," he said. He went home with Billie Jean. She heard him outside talking. He was telling Hazel that he soon would follow her. In six short weeks, Roy took that second heavenly flight that the man of God saw. (He wouldn't have wanted it any other way.)

Hazel was gone but never would she be forgotten! She had left behind a legacy that would never die. Not only had her life touched the people of her church; it had touched the townspeople. One doctor said, "Not only did Sis. Simpson leave a beautiful church for a memorial, her works stand for a memorial, also." Another doctor remarked, "Millington will never the same."

Hazel had left a legacy that those who follow would truly find her faithful. Her ministry not only touched the church, but it spread into the community and surrounding communities, towns, cities, counties, states, regions, countries, continents. It crossed all the barriers of humanity. Yes, Hazel was a truly a missionary at heart in every capacity!

She left the church in good financial condition. God had truly blessed her every effort. There was almost enough money in the treasury to pay for that new gym.

Our present Pastor, Rev. Travis Sheppard, did a tremendous job building the gym – complete with kitchen facilities, youth chapel, and evangelist's quarters. The present worth of the five acres and facilities are in excess of one million dollars.

On September 25, 1994, Pastor Sheppard held a Memorial Service in her honor. This date was five days short of the 10th anniversary of her passing.

It was a joyous occasion for many of her "children." Those attending were only a "drop in the bucket" compared to her many converts. The African-American, Indian, and Mexican races were well represented at this service – a token of her love for all mankind. All parking spaces were taken and many parked on the grass.

The Church was beautifully decorated with a large basket of cut flowers from the Trujillo family as well as silk roses from the McPeak family. Banners on the walls declared, "The righteous shall be in everlasting remembrance." (Psalms 112:6)

The sanctuary was bustling with excitement as many testified of the wonderful healings experienced in their lives as a result of her prayers and the wonderful name of Jesus, which was her first love. This Name was exalted as her granddaughter, Shiela Mullins, told of being born without an ankle bone and how God healed her as an infant, sparing her surgeries and corrective shoes. Her son, Delward, testified of a miraculous healing of a fractured leg that he had experienced. Joyce Laird told how the power of God healed her when doctors said she could never bear children. She held her grandbaby as she testified.

Rev. T. Richard Berford testified how he picked up Carrie

Mean's finger that had been cut off, and carried in a handkerchief to the doctor who sewed it on. Her finger turned black because her body rejected it. The doctor later took it off and threw it in the waste basket and bandaged her hand. When the bandage was taken off, she had a new finger. Glory to God!

Rev. Billy Watkins told of her desire to be a Missionary. Even though she would never fulfilled this desire, she had converts all over the world and served her generation faithfully.

Rev. Daniel Smith, who "stood in for his father," Rev. Harold Smith, told of the beautiful prayer meetings he remembered as a child when she came to his home. He told how Mike, his baby brother, had his arm broken. Daniel saw the bone sticking through the skin on his brother's arm. They propped him up with pillows and called Sis. Simpson to pray for him. Mike was out playing ball againt the next day because God healed him. Daniel remarked, "She's the greatest lady I ever knew." He then sang a song in her honor.

Rev. "Teddy" Ross, who held fiery revivals at the first little church and saw many baptized, spoke of her greatness. He stated that not every person makes God so special as she did. "She had Him up in first place, brother. I shall never forget the days and nights of revival here, of her long time in prayer. I think about her ministry being not effective only in Millington, but among the missionaries and all over the wide world." He stated that it will take judgment day to reveal all her greatness. "In honor of her today, I think one of the greatest choices God ever made for the state of Tennessee, he made in her. We are honored to be here and honor her today."

Many testimonies from pastors, evangelists, and the elders of the church told of the great influence that she had on their lives. Each person placed a silk rose in a vase after he finished speaking except Deacon Thomas C. Warren, who gave his rose to Delward Simpson, her son. The other roses were tied with a red ribbon and presented to Brenda Simpson, her daughter-in-law. The granddaughters also received roses.

This service was a reminder of the beautiful life she lived and how it touched others.

Delward thanked Pastor Sheppard and the church for their expressions of love and assured them how much his mother had loved them.

The speaker for the occasion was Bro. David Johnson, son of Rev. Don Johnson, pastor, recording artist, and chairman of the Assemblies of the Lord Jesus Christ.. Bro. David spoke on "Greatness." He pointed out attributes of greatness in each letter of the word - G R E A T.

The choir sang, "Old Country Church," as slides were presented showing the progression of the church from the first humble building to the modern sanctuary today – a span of 28 years.

The excitement continued throughout the three-hour service and it seemed folks didn't even want to leave – reminder that *"the memory of the just is blessed."* (Proberbs 10:7)

Hazel and Roy Simpson

A view of the sanctuary as saints gather in around the front of the church. (Pastor and Sis. Sheppard in the center front.)

Graduation time is a special time at the H.M. Simpson Academy. Pictured is Mark Sheppard receiving his diploma from his father, Pastor Sheppard.

A Tribute to
Rev. Hazel M. Simpson

She was a shepherd completely formed of God.

- Like Noah - she warned the people.
- Like Moses - she led God's flock.
- Like Abraham - she was faithful.
- Like Daniel - she prayed morning, noon, and night.
- Like David - she praised and worshipped her God.
- Like Isaiah - she prophesied to the people (spiritual gifts).
- Like Jeremiah - she wept for Zion.
- Like Solomon - she had wisdom from above (James 3:17).
- Like John the Baptist - she decreased and God increased.
- Like Peter - she preached Acts 2:38 (apostles doctrine Acts 4:12).
- Like John, the Revelator - she leaned on the Lord's breast in love and looked for the New Jerusalem coming down from God out of heaven.
- Like the heroes of faith in Hebrews 11 - she died in faith and loved not her life unto death.
- Like Paul - she wanted to know the Lord, and the power of His resurrection, and the fellowship of His suffering, being made conformable unto His death. She fought a good fight, she finished her course, and kept the faith. Henceforth, there is laid up for her a crown of righteousness which the Lord, the righteous judge, will give her at that day.

(II Timothy 4:8)

By Rev. Mike Edmaiston

OUTREACHES IN THE CHURCH

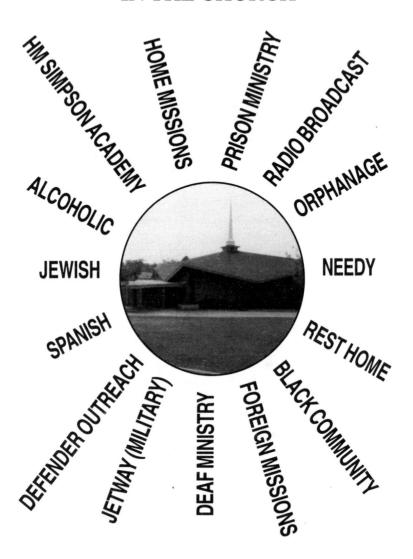

HM SIMPSON ACADEMY · HOME MISSIONS · PRISON MINISTRY · RADIO BROADCAST · ORPHANAGE · NEEDY · REST HOME · BLACK COMMUNITY · FOREIGN MISSIONS · DEAF MINISTRY · JETWAY (MILITARY) · DEFENDER OUTREACH · SPANISH · JEWISH · ALCOHOLIC

This little country girl, with an eighth grade education, had touched her world.

TO GOD BE THE GLORY!

Lets Look at Her Works
which Praise Her God . . .

PENNSYLVANIA PUERTO RICO MISSISSIPPI ARKANSAS CALIFORNIA WEST VIRGINIA ALASKA INDIANA JAPAN TEXAS FLORIDA JAMAICA LOUISIANA HIGH SEAS OKINAWA WISCONSIN TENNESSEE

For you see your calling, brethren, how that not many wise men after the flesh . . . are called . . . That no flesh should glory in His presence.
(I Corinthians 1:26-29)

Oh, What a Heritage!

We Remember Hazel . . .
(the miracles continue)

Chapter 13

WE REMEMBER HAZEL

*"The Righteous shall be in
everlasting remembrance . . ."*
Psalms 112:6

Billie Jean remembers . . .

"She was a wonderful mother who was always there for me. She always knew how to make me feel good about myself. She was always strong. Her love was genuine. I was so privileged to have a mother like her."

Delward Lee Simpson remembers . . .

"Dear Mom,

"I just want to drop you a few lines to let you know how much I love you and also to let you know that you were the best mom in world.

"You were never too busy to spend some time with me, and when I was in need, you were always there, even with your busy schedule.

"When I was in the Air Force, I could look for a letter from you every day. I have felt your special prayers for me throughout all my life.

"Each time I sit down to a meal, I remember your Bible studies and teaching of the Bible which have stuck with me all my life. 'Always remember no one can deceive you about God's word if you know it.'

"You are the dearest friend I have ever had. Like I say, I can always count on you for everything, even without asking.

"In closing, I want to say again, you are the dearest person that ever came into my life. I just can't tell you how much I appreciate you. Very few children were blessed with a mother like you. I also appreciate your love for everyone that you came in contact with. You never thought of yourself, always other people. Have a wonderful day up in Heaven.

Delward and Brenda Simpson

"Your loving son, Delward Lee."

Brenda Simpson (daughter-in-law) remembers . . .

"She was the dearest mother-in-law a person could have. She was also my pastor who was always there to encourage me. I always admired her and looked up to her. I knew she would always be there for me, anytime we needed her, day or night to help us and to pray for us when we were sick.

"She was so busy that we wouldn't call her sometimes, but the Lord would show her anyway just what we needed. She is really missed we loved her dearly."

Cherryl (granddaughter) remembers . . .

"My grandmother was a very special person in my life. I was her first granddauther. She use to tell me that I was just like her when she was young and looked like her too.

Cherryl remembers her grandmother as a friend.

"When I was twelve years old, I had a very traumatic experience happen to me. It caused an emotional crisis in my life. God showed my grandmother that I needed special attention. She carried me places, bought things for me, and always encouraged and uplifted me. She let me know that she would always be there for me. I really loved her, she was my friend, and I miss her very much.

Her granddaughter Debbie Rose remembers . . .

"My grandmother left a great heritage. She was a giant! Her strong faith was always there to touch God for my needs. She was the greatest influence in my life. I loved her very much."

Her granddaughter Sheila Mullins remembers . . .

"Grandparents have great influence on their grandchildren. My grandmother was a 'Prayer Warrior' who had a great influence on my life. She had great faith in God and knew how to encourage me when the outlook was

Pictured (right) is Sheila Mullins with Hazel's great-granddaughter Camela.

gloomy. When she told me it would be alright, it always was.

"I went with her to the conference and everywhere we went, she witnessed. She witnessed to the cab drivers, at the restaurants, and at the hotel. People listened to her. Her words touched them. Her phone was always ringing, because she got results.

"When my husband and I were on the field evangelizing, we saw many wonderful things like she told us. She left me a wonderful heritage. THANK GOD FOR MY WONDERFUL GRANDMOTHER!"

(Sheila Mullins attends Bethel United Pentecostal Church Memphis, Tennessee)

Lois Gill remembers . . .

"Sis. Simpson was such a wonderful pastor who taught the plan of salvation, the standard of holiness, and how to trust God. She always went to God. She taught us how to touch God for our needs. I'm so grateful for having been under her ministery. She certainly was the very best!

Roy Ross remembers . . .

"She had such great compassion."

Sharon Ross remembers . . .

"If there was one word to describe her it would be HUMBLE because she never lifted up herself; she always lifted up the Lord."

Tommy Warren remembers . . .

"She had always told me, "Keep your eyes on God, not on people because God will never fail you but people will."

Pat Warren remembers . . .

"Before I ever even thought about getting in church,

we would pass the little store-front building on Shelby Road on our way home from eating out on Sundays. I would see all the people there and feel so sorry for them because they had to worship in that building. I remember thinking, I wished I could help them in some way. I never dreamed that one day I would be worshipping with these very people! I have never known anyone with such a love for souls. She would go the second mile!"

Johnnie Vernon remembers . . .

"Sister Simpson left me with such good memories. One of the most outstanding things I remember about her, as an older teenager, was watching her on the platform weeping for her people, saved and lost. I remember thinking, what a burden she carries! It upset me to see her cry so hard. As an adult, I now understand that we must also have the same concern for souls.

"She was a beautiful landmark, and we must go back to the landmark that she left and be the examples that she taught us to be. We must be men and women with backbone enough to say, 'I will not look to the left nor to the right' when life deals me hardships. We must stand strong and trust God. He is always right on time.

"She instilled the truth in me and a deep love for God. As a teenager, I walked alone many times, but I knew she was always there for me anytime I needed her, day or night. I love God even more today than I did then.

"Today, I miss her more than ever. My love for her will never die. Thank God, she wasn't afraid to go on visitation and invite our large family to church. As an adult with children of my own, I'm glad she obeyed God. I want to do the same and see her again one day. It's not hard when you think of the great rewards."

Kay Willingham remembers . . .

"Like Deborah, she was a Mother in Israel who portrayed genuine love. She loved her members so much that she actually felt the pain of every member. The wayward members received the same love as those who were committed. Her love was unconditional.

Micah Dale Turner remembers . . .

"Sis. Simpson was a pastor who was like a grandmother. As a child, I noticed that when she corrected her members, she did it in a humble, loving way so that one would not be offended."

Thomas Adair remembers . . .

"I was raised in a Baptist church. My wife and children started going to Sis. Simpson's church, and my wife was filled with the Holy Ghost. Then I started attending with her and our children.

"When I first started going, I thought the men looked like most other men, but the women had real real long hair and no makeup. I asked myself, 'What kind of folks are these folks?' They ran in church and spoke in a language I could not understand. I just had to go back.

"After about two years, I would go to the men's prayer room. They would all pray. Then they would pray for one another. I soon learned what Pentecost was all about. I will always love and remember Bro. and Sis. Simpson.

"It was at the small church on Wilkinsville Road where God delivered me from the habit of smoking. I had tried to quit a lot of times and had been prayed for a lot of times. But the night that I went to Sis. Simpson, she prayed for me. She told me, 'God is no respecter of persons, what He will do for one, He will do for another.' I have never wanted another cigarette from that night on.

"I attended the church a long time. I thank God for her teaching and for all my brothers and sisters in the church. She always taught us that God puts a hedge around His own. You could feel the presence of the Lord just being around her as she talked and prayed. I thank God every day that my wife and children were all filled with the Holy Ghost under her teaching.

"A year or two went by and I was working at the Raleigh Fire Department. As I started to leave, my brother drove up on a small motorscooter that he had bought for one of his boys. After we visited and he started to leave, I cautioned him to be careful. He laughed and said he would. (He had owned a large motorcycle before.)

"I left and about 5:00 p.m. my boss called at home and said my brother, Aubrey Adair, had an accident and that I should go to the hospital at once. I called Sis. Simpson. She went with my wife and me to the hospital and she prayed all the way. When we arrived, all my family was there. Aubrey's wife, Helen, told us that he had had a really bad wreck. The doctor, who was a brain specialist, told us that he had a skull fracture and brain concussion and was critical.

"We all went into the prayer room. The spirit of the Lord filled that room. Sister Simpson asked God to heal him, but she said, 'If it be Thy Will.' We were told that if he pulled through the night, that it would be a miracle. He was unconscious 27 or 28 days. The doctors said that if he lived he would be a vegetable. We continued to pray, and I asked everyone I saw to pray for him.

"When he regained consciousness, the doctors told Aubrey that by all medical records he should have been a dead man the night he was admitted to the hospital. He added, 'Your brain was like a spider webb when the other doctors and I tested you at 11:00 o'clock that night. You should be a dead man.' I thank God for Sis. Simpson and everyone who prayed for him that night. Aubrey got out of the hospital and went back to work before his head was healed up.

"I, Thomas Adair, know that God did miracles before then and after, too. I thank God for all my brothers and sisters in the church. We will always remember Sis. Simpson and love her teachings until God carries us to be with her. I am thankful to share my testimony and be a part of this book.

Helen Adair remembers . . .

"Words fail to tell how much Sis. Simpson meant to me. God performed miracles when she prayed for me.

"I remember when my husband, Aubrey, had a wreck on a motor scooter that he was bringing home for our oldest son, Larry. The doctors told me he wouldn't live through the night, that his brain was scrambled like a spider's web. Sis. Simpson came to the hospital to be by my side. When she came out of the prayer chapel, she told me, 'He's going to live, and he will be alright.' The doctors had said, 'If he lives, he will just be a vegetable.' But I believed what God told my pastor. When Aubrey came out of the coma, he returned to work as usual. To God be the Glory!"

Jeanne Kaminski remembers . . .

"When I was 17 years old, something happened that left a great impression on my life. I will never forget the time when I was, in all my youthful ignorance, worrying about getting married soon. I went over to Sis. Simpson's house to pray with my mother about a guy that I was dating. When Sis. Simpson prayed for me, the Lord spoke through her and said, 'My child, I am preparing a son for you, he will come from a far land and I have chosen him above the others for you to do a great work in my kingdom.'

"I am now 31 years old and happily married to a wonderful husband from the far off land of Germany! I think about that often, even though at the time, I didn't understand. Looking back on that time in my life, I realized that I gained more than faith from Sis. Simpson's life. The Lord used her so mightily in prophecy."

(Jeanne Kaminski now attends World of Pentecost Church, Nanimo, British Columbia, Canada)

Janet Mitchell remembers....

"My husband was out of town. We had just moved, and I didn't have a car or a telephone. I had an attack of kidney stones. I was so sick and hurting so bad, that I went to Sis. Freddie Turner's house for prayer. She lived nearby. If anyone would have seen me, they would have thought that I was drunk because I was staggering down the street. When I got there, Sis. Simpson and Sis. Durham were at her house! They all prayed for me and God instantly healed me. I had had them several times and was hospitalized. I know that the pain just doesn't go away instantly. It was a miracle."

(Janet Mitchell is youth leader at Frayser Apostolic Church Memphis, Tennessee)

Van White remembers . . .

"Sis. Hazel Simpson was my rock. I was only three years old when I met this great Mother in the Lord. Some might even say I was too young to remember, but they are very wrong.

"She had such an impact on everyone she met - how could anyone forget?

"When I got sick I wanted her hands on my head because every time she prayed for me God healed.

"I could never explain how I felt about this great woman of faith. She taught me what was right and what was wrong. Nobody can ever take that from me.

"At four and a half years old, I received the Holy Ghost.

She encouraged me to learn the scriptures. My mother would help me memorize whole chapters at a time then Sis. Simpson would stand me on the altar and let me quote them. Oh, she made me feel so important!

"I look back on her with much admiration. I wish she were here now. I need her so. I just want to say. 'Thanks, Sis. Simpson,' even though she has already gone on to be with the Lord.

"You are not forgotten."

Michael Hegwood remembers . . .

"I was a young man raised under Hazel Simpson's teaching and preaching. My entire youth centered around her belief in God and the desire to please God with holiness and truth. My life after her death had taken me away from the goal she had for all of her congregation, which was heaven! I have experienced many trials that I didn't know how to handle. I was in situations where the devil had me believing that what I was taught was a good life but not necessary. He used this to steal my birthright, which was the ever present spirit of God and His protecting angels in my life leading me to the placed called heaven. Somewhere along the way, I began to recall the teachings of Sis. Simpson and found my way to a Pentecostal altar. God restored my life and now I am doing God's work, living and teaching the way Sis. Simpson lived and believed – that was prayer, fasting, and reading the Word of God. Thank you, Sis. Simpson, for the standard, the love, and the faith you had.

Sis. Simpson taught us to
"suffer the little children and forbid them not,
to come unto me . . ."

Benjamin Blevins remembers . . .

"Years ago we had an earthquake tremor in Millington. It shook our house. I was so scared, I thought it was a big man shaking our house. Sis. Simpson taught so strongly on baptism and the infilling of the Holy Ghost, that I told my Mom and Dad, 'I want the Holy Ghost, so if that big man gets me, I can go to heaven with Jesus.' We had church that night and I ran to the altar. I immediately started speaking in tongues. (My mother remembers me praying in tongues for over 30 minutes.) I was only four years old! My parents wondered if I was too young to be baptized. Sis. Simpson said, 'He wasn't too young for the Lord to give him the Holy Ghost,' and she baptized me in Jesus name!"

Roy Berford remembers....

"If ever I saw someone that was like Moses, it was Sis. Simpson. She had the meekness and quietness of a true shepherd. She was like a rock. She stood firm with her belief. Her life backed her up.

"You could call her anytime, day or night. She was touched by your needs, physical or spiritual. She would come with a prayer on her lips, before she reached your door. When she came through the door, you could feel the presence of the Lord. You just knew that your need would be answered.

"No matter how big the congregation was, everyone was special to her. She manifest the characteristics of the Lord. The life that she lived was the assurance to me that what she taught, preached, and prayed, was true."

Brenda Galloway remembers . . .

"Sis. Simpson was truly the greatest pastor that ever lived. My testimony is already in the pages of this book, but as a final tribute to my Mother in the Lord, I just want to say she was one of the greatest women of faith that

I've ever encountered. She taught me many things that I still hold dear to my heart and cherish.

"First of all coming straight from the Church of Christ to Pentecostal pews, it was hard for me to accept faith that my God could and would heal. But this woman, whose price is far above rubies, carried me around with her and through her I found that Jesus Christ was the same yesterday, today, and forever.

"Sis. Simpson has gone on now, but she'll live on in our hearts and minds as long as this world exists.

"Thank you for your teaching. You are as alive in my heart as you ever were. I love you."

Joanna Manley remembers....

"One of the first things that really stands out to me happened in 1979. I had gone water skiing with friends. Sis. Simpson had no idea where I was. She was praying in the afternoon and saw me in a boating accident. She called my mother, and asked her where I was? My mother told her that I had gone to a lake water skiing. It was about 1:00 p.m. Sis. Simpson told her what she had seen, and for her to join in prayer and plead the blood for my life!

"When I arrived home, at first I was afraid to tell my mother, what had happened to me. I knew it would worry her. Come to find out, that at the same time they were praying, this is what was happening to me.

"I was water skiing and fell off the skis. Another boat ran right over the top of me. I had on a life jacket, which should have kept me from going under the water. The driver of the boat that I was on, saw the boat and motor run over me, he just knew that I was dead. When I came back up, he knew it was a miracle from God! This happened at 1:00 p.m.!

"The next thing that happened, is still affecting my life

today. Two other young ladies and I were traveling to the conference with Sis. Simpson. As young girls seemingly do, we were discussing marriage! Sis. Simpson's usual time to pray was at 6:00 a.m., which she still did in the motel room. A prophecy was spoken through her, to me, for me not to look to the left or right but that the Lord could bring as far as the east and the west together and that I would have joys that I had never known. After this message came out, Sis. Simpson told me that she saw the name DAVID. Little did I know that three years later I would marry a man named DAVID!

"We married on June 30, 1984. We were the last couple that Sis. Simpson married. During the wedding she gave forth a message over us, that He had put us together to do a great work. After the ceremony she came, knelt, and prayed over us. Direct prophecy came out, that she saw an abundance of fish. And that we would be fishers of men. She said, 'I see rivers of fish and you are drawing them in.' She said, 'David, you have great faith, and I cannot begin to tell you the things that he has for you in your life'."

(Joanna and David Manley pastor at Rosemark. The Lord also uses him mightily in the word of prophecy. Their church has recently experienced four cancer healings, a young lady healed of Multiple Schlerosis, and a baby healed of a heart condition which would have required surgery.)

Donna Columbus remembers . . .

"At my wedding rehearsal, 14 years ago, Sis. Simpson prophesied over John and myself, 'That we would do a great work.' (John wasn't even called to the ministry yet.) Later she told us that she felt the same prophesy during the wedding ceremony.

"Little did we know that nine years later we would be

pastoring a church! Even though she was not alive during the time of our pastoring, she influenced John more than anyone. When situations would arise that he didn't know what to do, he'd say to me, 'Donna, what would Sis. Simpson say or do in this situation?' I would say, 'Just pray, because that's what I knew she would do about everything that happened.' This was a daily thing in our pastoring!"

(John and Donna Columbus pastored Soul's Harbor in Trenton, Tennessee for five years.)

Linda Jones remembers . . .

"I thought highly of my pastor, Sis. Simpson. I had the utmost repsect for her and confidence in her judgment. She was like a mother to me.

"God was moving on my husband to start a church in Covington, Tennessee. It was difficult for me to leave the security of the nice home church in Millington and start all over again in an old building where snow came through the cracks. The only help would come from the home church in Millington. At that time I was in my early 20s and had four small children, and a sick mother to care for. I was battling this when God gave me a dream. In this dream, I was looking out the picture window of my home where a tent was being erected for a revival when all at once this bright, beautiful, star appeared. I said, 'A star in the morning?' A voice spoke and said, 'Notice the direction the start is coming from.' I replied, 'from the north, up toward Covington.' The voice replied, 'I have given this to you.' This dream gave me the courage I needed to start the church there.

"We hadn't been there long when Michael, our baby, got real sick. He had loss of sight and difficulty breathing. Sis. Simpson prayed for him and God healed him.

"God filled many with the Holy Ghost and many were

baptized. We saw God do great things.

"One day, my husband started hemorrhaging from his mouth and nose until the sink was filled with blood. We called Sis. Simpson. When she prayed for him over the phone, he was healed.

"My daughter, Tina, was healed of yellow juandice and a piece of lead was removed from my son's, Donald Ray, leg as a result of prayer.

"My mother had been sick off and on for 15 years. She would get to death's door and then bounce back time and again. I was caring for her in my home. I was thankful each time God touched her.

"One night, when she was very low and the doctor had said, 'Call the family in,' God touched her once again. I questioned, 'Lord, why do you keep healing my mother?' I heard a voice say, 'Because you built a church for my Name's sake.'

"I raised my hands and started walking through the house praising God. I walked out on the front porch praising Him. I didn't care who saw or heard me even though it was around midnight. I must have felt like Blind Bartimaeus when he was crying out to Jesus and refused to be quieted! I was so thankful to serve a God with such love for me. I thank God for letting us build the church at Covington. We saw mighty moves of God there."

(Two other churches have been established as a result of that church. Praise the Lord!)

Carlene Ragsdale remembers:

"I am so thankful that I had the privilege of knowing Sis. Hazel Simpson. I couldn't begin to tell you what she has meant to me. She was a blessing to my life and to my family. She was always there for us anytime, day or night, regardless of the need.

"She taught a good standard of holiness, as well as to

pray always and to get the Word of God in us. Her life was a light to my pathway. I look forward to walking on those streets of gold with her.

"May God bless you Sis. Hazel Simpson for helping me, but most of all for baptizing my Mother in the Name of Jesus, just a few weeks before she died. Thanks for visiting her at the hospital before God called her home. Because of you, I believe she is rejoicing with the angels in heaven and dancing on streets of gold there with you. Thank you so very much."

June Basham remembers . . .

"Jesus has done many wonderful things for me since He filled me with the Holy Ghost and I was baptized in Jesus' Name. I could literally fill a book with the things He has done for me, but I will just tell you a few of the highlights.

"God sent a young man in the navy to my church who very shortly afterwards received the Holy Ghost and was baptized in Jesus Name. Oh, how God moved so quickly! We were soon going together, and God showed us that we were meant for each other. God even performed a wedding miracle for us. Our wedding date had been set, announcements sent out, announcement placed in newspaper - everything was set. Then, Jim's commanding officer (who had to write a chit for Jim to get leave to come to the wedding) was sent out of town on emergency leave. They didn't know when he would be back. Jim called me and said we would have to postpone the wedding until his commander got back in town. I told Him, 'No, that if God really meant for us to get married, He would make a way.' Jim's officer came back in town on Friday; Jim got the chit signed and was at the church by noon Saturday. The wedding was at 7:00 that night. A miracle, yes, indeed!

"The doctors said I could not have children. I was

lead to read how Sarah in Genesis 17 had conceived in her old age; so, I prayed and knew that God had answered. It's not old age at 35, but certainly not the usual child-bearing age. I was blessed with both a girl and a boy, and now I have three grandchildren.

"Another miracle God performed was when Jim had a wreck in his semi-tractor trailer. The doctors said he wouldn't live. I prayed, called my pastor, Sis. Simpson, and had the church pray for Jim. After seeing Jim in the emergency room, I returned home that night and was pray-ing. The Lord spoke to me and told me Jim would live but would lose sight in his right eye. It happened exactly that way. Jim lived and worked for 2 1/2 more years. After that accident, God did many more miracles for Jim and I. He healed Jim of pneumonia after the doctors said he would not make it through. But God did come through, once again, as He always has! He is so faithful."

Charlotte Carlisle remembers . . .

"I came to Sis. Simpson's revival seeking the Holy Ghost. My Mom had been a great witness to me and taught me that I must have it. I had seen God do so many miracles through her that I knew I wanted this for myself and my family.

"After two nights at her revival, God filled me and my two sons with the Holy Ghost. My son, Billy Wayne, spoke in tongues the rest of the night.

"I was delivered from a habit of smoking that I had had since I was 18. I came home from church that night, and as usual, I lit a cigarette and started to smoke, but it made me so sick that I have never wanted another one.

"I did not drive then, so Sis. Simpson would pick me up for church or any other place that I needed to go. She encouraged me to learn to drive and with her prayers and encouragement, I decied to take driver's training.

"If there was a need of any kind, day or night, she

would be there with her prayers and encouragement. Many times she prayed over the phone.

"She always esteemed others above herself. Her day began at 6:00 a.m. at the church praying for everyone, calling their names in prayer.

"Once, when my son, John, got his arm cut badly, I rushed him to her house, and when she prayed, the blood stopped and he didn't need stitches.

"Another son got involved with drugs in high school. The doctors at the rehabilitation center said it would take three years for him to lose his desire for drugs. Even though he wanted to be free, he was hooked. I had faith that God could do it sooner.

"Sis. Simpson and I would go to these apartments where all these young people were 'strung out' on drugs. We prayed for them and talked to the ones we could talk to and brought my son to the church where he could pray for deliverance. Most people would have been afraid to enter these apartments, but not her because she knew her God was a deliverer! It took my son one year to be free.

"My heart will ever be greateful for a lady who loved me and taught me that God's Word is true, that God is greater than any problem, and that His Spirit would guide us if we obey.

Hank Whitsitt remembers . . .

"When I first met Hazel Simpson, the pastor of the United Pentecostal Church in Millington, Tennessee, I was somewhat critical of her. Her physical appearance alone did not evoke admiration or respect. In fact, I found her rather plain to look at. Then on top of that - a woman preacher! Being analytical by nature, I scrutinized her teachings with skepticism for flaws which would discredit her in my personal view. I could not believe anyone could be so committed to religion by choice. What could possibly be in it for her? As time passed, I became increasingly impressed with her teachings which followed the Bible precisely. She used the 'Word of God' with enthusiasm and always in proper context. She wielded it like a sword, with authority given her by God Himself. She usually displayed a jubilant demeanor but was always serious when it came to God and His salvation plan. She would quickly rebuke anyone in her presence who displayed the slightest disrespect toward God, then turn right around and cry genuine tears of joy over someone's good fortune or blessing from God.

"She had a deeper, more extraordinary sense of God's will revealed through the Bible. This unique insight apparently dictated that her life be fully subordinate to God. Hazel Simpson actually lived what she preached. She loved the Bible and could quote scripture on and on from memory. No scripture was ever hidden from her.

"I developed a deep respect and loving admiration for her as time went on. She had been very patient with me. I feel, probably like all of her 'children,' that she had a special interest in me as she would single me out for in depth tutoring in scriptures. It was as if she was trying to prepare me for some unknown eventuality. By this time I was convinced she was right, and I listened and studied intently.

"I finally gave over my stubborn will and God filled me with a portion of His Spirit. Through it all, I received a special insight to the Word of God, not just what the words read but the essense or spirit of the word and the elation and excitement that comes from knowing the Great God saw fit to call me His own in a very personal way. It is an experience that is indelibly marked in my memory. It has never faded and when I take the time to consider it, a flood of emotion rises up within and tears of joy fill my eyes no matter where I am.

"I am convinced that were it not for Hazel Simpson, I

would have continued on with life without God or knowing the joy of His love. I recognize Hazel Simpson as my spiritual Mother. But she preferred me to call her 'Sister Simpson' and I do in respect and loving memory of her. God bless her!"

Sue Whitsitt remembers . . .

"I've never been good at expressing myself with fancy words, but to me Sis. Simpson meant love, warmth, honesty, caring, always a friend, and a spiritual leader. I could always depend on her to pray for and with me; God answered her prayers. I love her and miss her very much."

Sheila (Rodgers) Sutherland remembers . . .

"When asked if I'd like to contribute to this memorial of truly one of the finest ladies and pastors that ever lived, my first thoughts were how could I ever come up with the words that could even come close to describing the outstanding woman that she was or the lasting impact that she has had on my life.

"When I first met Sis. Hazel Simpson, as a young teenager that had just prayed through to the Holy Ghost, I can remember sitting in awe during church services watching this lady pastor as she would remain caught up in the Spirit of God from the beginning of each service until its very end. I often said that I believe this woman speaks in 'tongues' more than she does in English (which included outside the four walls of the church as well as in)!

"The pages would be endless if I were to elaborate on all the beautiful memories that I will forever cherish in my heart, and the wonderful times that I was so privileged to have been able to share with this precious lady whom I was proud to call my pastor.

"One year, Corrine Adair and I went to campmeeting

with Sis. Simpson in Perryville, Tennessee. After we had traveled a few miles down the road, she said to us, 'Girls, let's pray and ask the Lord to keep His guiding hand upon us on our trip.' Well, knowing this prayer warrior like I did, I wasn't too awfully surprised when I looked up just in time to see both hands leave the steering wheel as she raised them toward heaven and prayed to her God. She had the utmost confidence and faith to believe that no matter what, He would always be right there to provide her every need. It wasn't long before the Spirit of God began to fill and saturate that bronze colored 1977 Lincoln Towncar. That day we had a Holy Ghost prayer meeting by just simply asking the Lord's protection while traveling on the highway.

"It's been over thirteen long years now since the Lord took her to what she often referred to as the 'Glory World,' and I still miss her dearly. She was not just as pastor and shepherd over her flock, but someone you could also call a friend. The hour never grew too late nor arose too early for her to, without hesitation, go to one of her sheep that was in need regardless of the circumstance. Just like the shepherd in the Bible that left the 99 to go find the one, she too, was always willing to go that extra mile.

"In the seven years that I was so blessed to have had her as my pastor, she re-baptized me, having been baptized previously as a young child many years before, performed the wedding ceremony for my husband and I, baptizing him as well, and dedicated our first two children to the Lord, as I was expecting my third child when the Lord called her home.

"I can truly say that I've never known another like her, nor has anyone ever touched or influenced my life the way she did. We cannot know all the answers to life's questions, nor can we always understand 'why.' But the Lord saw fit to take this tried and tested, yet precious jewel home where she now lives in her 'new body' that has never known one moment's pain since the day she arrived.

"I think one thing we could all agree on is that heaven is now more richly blessed with her there. I can almost see her now shouting up and down those golden streets and looking below to the rest of us, clapping her hands and singing, "Just wait till you see my brand new home!"

Rev. Alan Wilson remembers . . .

"Thirty-two years ago, I received the Holy Ghost under Hazel Simpson's ministry. I have been licensed and ordained to preach 30 of those years. I will never forget the basic teaching Sis. Simpson gave us. In fact, I still teach and believe it.

"Those of us who were fortunate enough to sit under her were truly blessed of God to be able to glean the truth she loved so well. The teaching on holiness standards have never left me and I still maintain them today.

"One unique characteristic Sis. Simpson had is a trademark for every pastor and that was she loved her people. After leaving and coming back to preach as an evangelist, I can remember hearing her praying all hours of the night, literally. Sis. Simpson was a woman of faith. The good Lord only knows how many people received their healing because Sis. Simpson let the Lord use her in this ministry.

"What patience this woman possessed when her church went from a handful to over a hundred in just a little while. She truly had a job on her hands. Most of us had not been in church and we had a lot to learn. God had the person there to teach us.

"Since I have been pastoring for the last 14 years, many times in prayer when I would be dealing with a wayward saint, I'd think about how much trouble I caused

Sis. Simpson and could do nothing, but again ask God to forgive me and give me the patience, the strength, the knowledge, and the wisdom to pastor my church as he did Sis. Simpson.

"I could go on and on but I know there are a lot of other tributes to be read so I'll close with this. While talking with another preacher the other day, he said, 'Bro. Wilson, the Lord's blessed you to get into your new church, your ministry is successful, you've got a lot to be thankful for.'

"This is true. But I've always said and want to say again, that if I'm successful, Sis. Simpson had a lot to do with it. If I fail, it won't be her fault because she taught us the truth and lived it to show us the example. I feel my ministry is an extension of hers. She was a special lady. There was only one Sis. Simpson.

Kathy Collins remembers . . .

"At age 19, I was married with one child. My husband was in the military and Millington was our first duty station. I had never been away from home before and was very lonely. My husband was always drinking and gambling. I felt all alone. I really didn't know the Lord personally, but I always prayed. I also prayed that the Lord would send me someone to talk to.

"One day there was a knock on the door. It was someone selling Avon. I couldn't afford to buy anything, but I invited her in anyway. I needed to talk to someone. After talking for awhile, she invited me to her church.

"When I first went to this church, I could feel the Spirit of God. I knew these people were on fire for the Lord.

"Things began to turn around once I started going to church. Well, not with my husband at first. I was in church every time the church doors were open. My daughter, Lana, would fall asleep on the pews because we would pray for so long.

"All of my religious background I must say came from Sis. Simpson and the Millington church. I was baptized and filled with the Holy Ghost here. I learned how to pray and humble myself unto the Lord. I also learned how powerful the Name of Jesus is. When you can call on His Name, He is there.

"I had a lot of respect for Sis. Simpson. She taught me how to be a godly young woman through the Word of God. I feel like Sis. Simpson planted seeds in my soul that I could never forget.

"When my husband and I got shipped out and I didn't get to another church right away; however, the foundation that Sis. Simpson gave me could never be forgotten. After awhile, I began to go out in the world, again. I always knew what was right and what wasn't because of my background.

"Now that I am truly with the Lord, again, I look back on my days at the Millington church, and I just thank God for sending me to Sis. Simpson and her church. My whole family is now on fire for the Lord."

Cindy (Smith) Johnson remembers . . .

"I have loving memories of my great aunt, Hazel Simpson, who loved me as a granddaughter. She always told me that I was part her because she had labor pains when I was born.

"As a child growing up, I found no problem was too small for her to take time to talk and pray with me. She gave all herself to everyone.

"The memories she left me were how to fast, pray, and have faith. I am so glad I had her to cry with me and pray with me. She even married my husband and me.

"Nanny, I wish my boys could have known you. They think they do because I tell them all about you. They tell their friends that you are their "Nanny" too! I wish with all my heart that you were here with me today, but I'm glad I can go to you someday. Save a spot for me, because I want to be next to you in heaven. I love you."

Dee Wells remembers.....

"I had the privilege of sitting under Sis. Simpson for about 13 years. During that time I was witness to many miracles, signs, and wonders that accompanied her ministry. Also, I was a recipient of her genuine love for the saints that God placed in her care.

"There are so many things that I could write about, but one instance really sticks out in my mind. It was just seven or eight months before the Lord took her on. It was just before she could no longer pastor full time because of the illness that was taking over her body. My oldest daughter, Vicky Keller, and myself were both very sick with a virus. We were experiencing upset stomachs, aches, chills, and fever. As was my practice in the past 13 years, I telephoned my pastor for prayer. She was already quite ill, and I asked her if she could just pray for us over the telephone. She did that, but soon I heard a knock at my door. There she stood in the cold and rain, very sick herself, but she had come to pray for us.

"We were living in a mobile home at that time. She came into our living room, knelt down in front of the couch and proceeded to get in touch with the Almighty God. Both my daughter and I were healed instantly when she anointed us with oil and prayed for us. The Holy Ghost permeated that room. I look back on it now and I feel that there was enough Holy Ghost in that little room to heal every disease that ever attacked mankind. Yet just a few months later she passed away, being taken over with cancer.

"She leaves a rich heritage behind her. She had all nine gifts of the spirit operating actively in her ministry. She taught us that if we would live for God, we could trust Him to heal our bodies as He has so many times. She taught us that it takes a dedicated life to make heaven.

"Bro. Benson, when he preached her funeral, said that if the Book of Acts were being written today she would have a part in it.

"There is a song that says something like, 'Will Those Who Come Behind Us Find Us Faithful?' My prayer is to be faithful, like the example that went before me."

(Dee Wells attends Lighthouse, Florence, Mississippi)

Faye Smith remembers . . .

"Sister Simpson was my aunt. I had always admired her, but when she started going to church, there was just something special about her.

"She witnessed to me about Jesus Name and told me how the God of the Old Testament became the Lord Jesus of the New Testament. It was a wonderful revelation.

"When I was fifteen years old, she told me about a dream she had. In this dream, a blond headed boy and a brown headed girl were going down this slippery path. They kept sliding off. She worked very hard to keep them on this path. Sometimes she would almost slide off herself keeping them on this path. I said, 'Aunt Hazel, the Lord just showed me that I am that girl.' I was only fifteen at the time, but later I married that blond headed boy and that dream came true.

"Her prayers helped us until we could stabilize and be strong enough to walk that straight and narrow pathway. She helped me trust God and become a strong minister's wife. It's because of her prayers and persistence that I am where I am today.

"One of the highlights of my life was when God spoke and said that He had put us together to pray. (When two agree, it shall be done.) We saw God do many miracles praying together. I thank God for my Aunt Hazel."

Celeste Bailey remembers . . .

"Sis. Simpson prayed more then anyone I ever knew. She was so dedicated. Her church was her whole life. When I was about five years old, I had warts all over my hands. She took my little hands in hers and prayed for them. I will never forget when I woke up the next morning; the warts were gone!

"When Bro. Mac and I traveled on the evangelistic field, everywhere we went people knew her for her faith, dedication, and prayer life."

(Celeste Bailey is the pastor's wife, Gospel Lighthouse Waupaca, Wisconsin)

Doris Berford remembers . . .

"In January of 1972, I took real sick. Sis. Simpson came out and prayed for me. A message from God was spoken out over me. God told me, 'You shall have the desires of your heart.'

"Sister Simpson told me that I was expecting a baby and that was why I was so sick. This was the last thing on our minds as we felt we already had all that God had in store for us in this order. Our baby was six years old. We had two girls, the oldest being nine years old at the time.

"My husband began to ask me if I even knew the desires of my heart. I told him that was no problem. Ever since I was a little girl being raised with a family of only four girls and no brothers, I always wanted a son and for him to look just like his dad. So when God told me I would have my desire fulfilled, I knew without a doubt I was to have a son

"Our beautiful baby boy was brought into this world on Oct. 3, 1972. He weighed 7 lbs. 2 oz. and was 17 1/2 inches long. He was very short like his mom. We took him for all the tests that babies have to have. The doctor said we had a fine healthy baby boy.

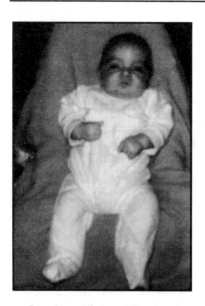

Stephen Richard Berford

"As soon as I was able, the first place I took him was to church, where he was dedicated to our wonderful Lord. God gave out another message that day. He said, 'I have given him to you to give back to me.' I thought, 'God here he is, use him in any way you see fit.'

"For two months and twenty-nine days we loved and enjoyed our beautiful baby. He grew to weigh 14 lbs. and looked just like his dad.

"On January 2, 1973, he took real sick. Sis. Simpson and a few more prayer warriors came out to our house to pray for him. As we prayed, (I found out later) Sis. Simpson said she felt a cool breeze blow across her legs. She looked to see if a vent was in the floor where air could creep in. She realized there were no vents there, even though she felt a breeze go across her leg. She knew she had prayed the angel of death away twice. The third time she felt it, God allowed the angel to take my baby home.

"Sister Simpson said she had a vision and saw him in a playground; he looked to be about 11 or 12 years old. She believed that that would be around the time we would see him again. On Sept. 30, 1984, God took Sister Simpson home to be with him. On Oct. 3, 1984 my beautiful baby boy, Stephen Richard Berford, would have been 12 years old.

"Since that time God has given me two wonderful

SONS-in-law and three beautiful grandSONS.

Rev. T. Richard Berford remembers . . .

"She was a mother in the Lord who was a great example, and a great leader who walked in the Spirit. I owe my 33 years of walking with God to her wise spiritual upbringing. In my opinion, she was a pastor who was unsurpassed."

Rev. Harold Smith remembers . . .

"I came to Memphis in 1957, shortly after my Mother died. I had been evangelizing and was looking for direction from God. Sis. Simpson met me at one of these revivals. She said, 'God has given you to me to pray for.' She became my spiritual Mother. I would not be where I am today had it not been for her teaching and prayers. I would pastor for a while and then return home to the Millington church. God sent us home one last time, for just a bit more teaching. She died six months after we took the church at Wesseson, Mississippi."

(Pastor Harold Smith, First Pentecostal Church, Marks, Mississippi)

Rev. Billy Watkins remembers . . .

"She was my pastor, my Mother in the Lord, who prayed always and not just at church. She and Bro. Simpson were the greatest people in the world. They treated me like their own son. They lent me their car.

"She was really concerned about others. Her love was genuine. She continued to check on people after she had prayed for them. She was persistent, a great prayer warrior, and a great minister who never exalted herself. God exalted her because she put others first and herself last.

"I remember the time when my son, Paul, was a baby.

He became very ill. We took him to the doctor, but he continued to run a high temperature for days. His little lips were turned out from the high fever. We took him to church and Sis. Simpson prayed for him. My wife took him back to her seat, but his temperature still hadn't gone down. Sis. Simpson walked from behind the pulpit, took him in her arms, and went into the back of the church. When she returned, he was completely well!"

Pastor Dolly Willingham remembers . . .

"I came in the old church on Shelby Road before it burned. It had pink walls and green carpet. There was an outhouse that leaned and was covered with a burlap bag. What a long way the present church came all because of Pastor Simpson's dream!

"I remember so many wonderful things, that I could never tell them all. I had headaches, really bad. After prayer, God healed me. Once I was paralyzed for weeks. I couldn't raise my arm. It was so paralyzed, that Bro. Willingham had to brush my hair and dress me. Sis. Simpson kept believing and prayed for me. The Lord healed me.

"One evening in service while Sis. Simpson was preaching, the Lord showed me that she had a tumor the size of a baseball in her stomach. I went up to her and told her what I saw. She said, 'The Lord had to have showed you, because no one knew about it but her, and she was trusting in the Lord to heal her.' We prayed together and God healed her!

"She never let satan hinder her. One night, during service, I looked toward the door and saw a giant man in the doorway. The only way that I know how to describe him was that he looked like the jolly green giant. He was very good to look upon. He had blond hair. He was wearing shorts with a bottle in his pocket. He stood, looking back and forth over the congregation. We knew it was the presence of satan. Sis. Simpson had the congregation start praying in fervent prayer. He just disappeared! Thereafter, we would enter the church, and rebuke the presence of satan from entering.

"I was traveling in West Virginia and was involved in a wreck. I tried to reach my pastor on the phone, but couldn't get through. I knew my jaw was broken. 'I told the Lord, if He would just heal me, I would use my mouth for him.' I drove on back to Millington. I went to the doctor. He took an x-ray and told me my jaw was broken. He wanted to wire it. I had Pastor Simpson pray for me. The Lord healed me!

"I have surely used my 'mouth' for the Lord since!

"We were more like sisters than 'natural kin.' She taught such great faith and trusting the Lord for healing. She taught the wonderful plan of salvation. The teachings she instilled in me are like my mother's. They continue on through my ministry today.

(Rev. Dolly Willingham, Emmanuel Temple, Covington, Tennessee)

Rev. Donald Gill remembers . . .

"My son brought me a piece of paper a few months ago and on it he had written a message called "Foundations." He said maybe I could preach it sometime.

"Of course, I cried when I read it because I was thinking that maybe God was placing a call on his life and that was one of my greatest dreams for him, that he would do something for Jesus. But when I began to read the message, my mind immediately went to a little woman who probably had more of an impact on my life than anyone besides Jesus. Sis. Simpson used God's Word to build a foundation in my life and my wife's and son's life that has taken us through many a storm and many a trial. There have been times when I thought the windows were falling out and the roof and walls were coming down, but when the dust settled, the foundation was still standing and I was right in the middle of it.

"Sis. Simpson inspired in me a desire to keep going when everything was crumbling around me. I have learned through the years that the teaching of God's Word, she helped to instill in us, has been a beacon and a lighthouse for all these years since her death. There would not be enough time to tell of the times she comforted us with a word from Jesus, or the times she, being led by the Holy Ghost, would encourage us to keep living for God.

"Of all the wonderful things and precious memories I have of her, I would want to say 'Thank You' for preaching the Word of God to me and teaching me holiness with love. I still miss her and I find myself thinking of her many times, but I realize she is better off and her rest is complete now that she has made it over Jordon.

"One last thing I would like to write is something that happened on the day we buried her. I don't know about others but I leaned on Sis. Simpson tremendously, and it was a crushing blow for me to lose her. But I saw a plaque on her office wall that said, 'Thy Word is a Lamp unto my Feet and a Light unto my Path.' God spoke to my heart at that time and told me if I was going to stand, I would have to get His Word in me through studying on my own and doing my own praying.

"Since that time I have read the Bible through many times, and God has enlightened me through His Word. Many times when I read certain scriptures, I smile and think to myself of how many times I had heard Sis. Simpson quote it. I still pray for her family and hope they will honor the great sacrifice she made for God and all of us.

"I have heard other preachers who could out-preach her, but I've never known a better Pastor in all my life. Thank you Jesus and thank you Sis. Simpson for all you have done."

(Rev. Donald Gill and family Sheila, Buddy, Kelly, and Savannah, Praise Tabernacle, Munford, Tennessee)

Rev. John Johnson remembers . . .

"As a young minister when I first arrived in Tennessee 15 years ago, I did not believe in women preachers until I began to talk to the Lord. The Lord showed me one night as I was sitting on the front pew. I saw a thick smoke around where Sis. Simpson was sitting and around where I was sitting. It went like a straight line from me to her. After service I went straight to her and told her what I had seen. She told me she saw it too! I told her what I had asked the Lord to show me. She smiled real big. I've never met anyone so filled and over-running with the affectionate Love of God as my pastor, Sis. Simpson.

"One night in the dead of the winter, I was sleeping on the top bunk of my trailer. A stong wind blew out the pilot light to my heater. Gas began to fill the trailer. I awoke to very strong fumes of butane gas. I felt a very sharp agonizing pain in my head. I realized tears were streaming down my face. I jumped in my van and went to Sis. Simpson's house. It was 3:00 a.m. when I knocked on the door. She opened the door and I walked straight to her prayer room. She came in with her little bottle of oil and said 'just believe Johnny' and laid her hand on my head. In seconds the pain was gone! I looked up and said to her 'it's gone.' She was still praising and thanking God for the healing and said, 'just praise God, Johnny for the healing.'

"I remember going to the hospital a couple of nights before Sis. Simpson passed away. I was very confused and puzzled because I could not understand why God would allow someone like her to suffer because of the faith and miracles that where in her life. She had trusted God for her healing all those years.

"My wife and I knelt and prayed. I saw the back of her walking through a dark sky as if it where night. Then all of a sudden, I was standing in front of her. The brightness of day was all around her. The Shekinah cloud of glory was waist high as far as you could see. When I looked at her face, she looked 20 years younger for the smile that lit her face. I did not see what she was beholding with her eyes, but I could only guess! Then and only then did I know how precious is the death of His Saints."

Rev. Donald De La Rosa remembers . . .

"About August 1974, in the the City of Millington, Tennessee, I had neighbors named Jane and Allen Gramlick. They invited my wife, Cecilia, to go with them to the First United Pentecostal Church of Millington. It was

The Don De La Rosa Family – Jennifer, Josie, Cecila, and Don.

funny and amazing at the same time how we came to the truth.

"Some time back we were looking for a church to attend and could not find one. One day a lady at the Navy relief thrift store located on the Naval base told us of a place in town to find clothes for our new born baby girl, Josie. So on this one Saturday, we set out to find this place to find clothes. We came to this church building with the name First United Pentecostal Church of Millington. (At that time we didn't know the difference in churches.) I didn't see a yard sale sign, so I looked in the basement to see if any kind of a sale was going on. As I looked inside the building, I heard this lady praying like I had never heard before. She was asking the Lord to help the lost people in Millington. I found out several days later that it was the pastor praying.

"My neighbors didn't know that my wife and I had already seen the church. When Cecilia came back that Sunday from going to church with the neighbors, she told me that it was the one we went to that Saturday and that the lady praying was the pastor. This was how I came into contact with Rev. Hazel Simpson.

"Sis. Simpson came to our apartment a few Saturdays later and told me that Jesus loved me and that He died for me and that He wanted to help me. She baptized me that Sunday when I went to church – the power of the Holy Ghost was all over the place. Jesus filled me with His precious Spirit the next Sunday. The Lord has helped me ever since.

"Sis. Simpson was the one that took me before the Tennessee District to get my local minister's license. She was very intrumental in the way I preach even to this day. I owe all the things that have happened in my life to this great woman that loved the Lord with all her heart, soul, mind, and specially, her strength. I have never met a more dedicated christian. In all the years of my attending different church throughout the UPCI, Sis. Simpson is still a model for the De La Rosa family.

"Cecilia was baptized by Sis. Simpson as well as my two lovely daughters Josie and Jennifer. God truly has looked out for my family that I love so much. God has healed the girls of different sicknesses. Josie was healed of polio when just a child there in the Millington church. Also, my baby girl, Jennifer, was healed of this lump on her neck. She still has a scar to show the mercies of the Lord. All this was done because of a woman that took the Word of God just like it said and never wavered.

"Today I still hold a license for the United Pentecostal Church and pastor a Spanish church in Norfolk, Virginia, where I am stationed in the United States Navy. I also hold the position as Elder at the First United Pentecostal Church of Norfolk, Virginia, where Rev. James Dunlap is my pastor.

"As I write this short testimony, I serve as lay leader for the United Pentecostal church on Board the United States Nuclear Carrier U.S.S. George Washington CVN-73. Several have come to knowledge of the truth because you guessed it . . . all due to a lady that didn't know the word "quit" or "it can't be done." Everything that I will do in the present or future will be added to this lady that I loved like a mother.

"Thank you, Sis. Simpson, for being the light that Jesus wanted you to be. I could never express the

Daniel and Josie Niculae

gratitude and love that you showed to me and several members of the military forces that were touched my your service to God.

"To end this testimony, I would like for you to know that Josie is still living for the Lord and can walk normal because of prayer. She is now married to Daniel A. Niculae of Norfolk, Virginia. Jennifer is still loving the Lord will all her heart and being used as a light for Jesus Christ in this time of trouble amoung our young adults in high school. My precious wife remains a pillar for God."

Jeff Hamilton remembers . . .

"When I think of Sis. Simpson, the most prominent thought that comes to mind is that she was the greatest example of a true Christian that I have ever known. In word and in deed, the character and attributes of Jesus Christ were personified through her every day life.

Jeff Hamilton at the Texas campgrounds.

"Sis. Simpson taught me of the faith that was delivered once to the saints. I will be forever thankful that she embraced that pure faith with insight and without compromise. Not only did she impart that faith to me but to everyone that had ears open to the voice of the Spirit.

"Through the ministry of Sis. Simpson, I became rooted in the true doctrine of the Word of God. Under the shadow of His wings of mercy, I grew strong in the Lord and developed a deep love for the truth. This foundation established me in the faith and has kept me for the last 17 years.

"Had it not been for Sis. Simpson standing in the gap and making the difference, God only knows what my fate would have been. I am so thankful to God that He used the U.S. Navy to take me from Brooklyn, NY, all the way to the little town of Millington, TN, to show me His gospel and give me a pastor who reflected Him, speaking the truth in love."

Linda Ross remembers . . .

"I remember Sis. Simpson as a role model. Today, her teaching still influences my life many years later. She was always doing good and helping others, anytime day or night, when they were in trouble or need.

"This lovely lady taught me to have faith in God for miracles. She believed there was nothing her God couldn't do. She convinced me that God's miraculous power is real today.

"On Dec. 13, 1994, at Jackson, Tennessee, General Hospital when two surgeons started the procedure to remove my gall bladder and a tumor in my ovary, they found cancer. They took a biopsy and closed me up. They didn't give me much encouragement. The tumor, the size of a large, odd-shaped cantaloupe, spit cancer cells out like taking your hand and sowing seeds. Cancer cells had landed on my liver and all over my body. Prayer was made and my pastor told me, 'This sickness is not unto death.'

"I was referred to a good cancer doctor in Memphis and started taking chemo. My family members and friends all over the world 'went to bat' for my life. They fasted and prayed, asking God for a miracle in my life. One dear friend told me, 'God has healed you.'

"The CAT Scan taken in June showed no sign of cancer. The CA 125 test showed up 7 (within the normal range).

"On August 9, 1995, when surgery was performed to remove the gall bladder, appendix, and ovaries, the surgeons found no tumor nor any cancer cells with the naked eye. All the biopsies turned out negative except my right ovary. Even though the ovaries were enlarged, there was no tumor or sign of a tumor. The biopsies of the lymph nodes, liquid in the lining of the stomach, and gall bladder were all negative. (The tumor had grown so large it extended to my rib cages before I was healed.)

"I praise and thank God for a miracle in my life and especially for my mother, my family, my church family, and all my friends who 'went to battle' for my life.

"Had it not been a dedicated woman like Sis. Hazel Simpson, we might not have known how to trust God for things in our life."

Donald and Delores Tucker remember . . .

"Sis. Simpson baptized us in 1965. I (Delores) received the Holy Ghost when I was baptized, and Don soon thereafter. I was a 22-year-old mother with four children and Don was only 25. These 29 years have been wonderful walking with God. We've never been sorry.

"Sis Simpson instilled a love for God's Word and Jesus' name in our hearts. She taught us how to worship God in spirit and in truth, and not to be church hoppers. She taught us to buy the truth and sell it not like the Bible says. She also taught us that prayers the key to heaven and Jesus is the solid rock. His names a strong tower that the rightous can run into and find safety. When my son, Tim, went into the army in 1982, it was a difficult time. I read my Bible and prayed daily and trusted God. God

Don and Delores Tucker

brought him home safetly . The teaching I got under Sis. Simpson has stood the test of time. Jesus never fails. We thank God for such a wonderful pastor."

Linda Cowan remembers . . .

"I almost feel as if I have cheated – I got a sneak preview when I started laying out this book.

"Oh, the memories! I have laughed, I have cried, and I have shouted. It has been a long time since my home has experienced such apostolic power. I needed to go back to my beginning, and this book has done that for me. I am so grateful and honored to be a small part of this great work! I truly believe that this book will encourage and uplift those of us that knew Sis. Simpson, but more important, I believe the pages within this cover will exalt the Almighty to those who have never experienced or manifested the Holy Ghost power the way Sis. Simpson did. Death has not robbed us – the wake that follows her death is full of heritage and her Godly legacy continues on. Prayers are eternal – Sis. Simpson put her dreams to prayer and they really do continue on . . . on in all the lives she has so gracefully touched.

"I have never know another human being quite like her. She was a great woman of God, but that greatness did not come without sacrifice. She gave a great sacrifice – herself totally. We have but to follow her example to experience that same spiritual depth.

"One of my fondest memories of Sis. Simpson was when I was attending a general conference with her in Kansas City, Missouri. I was so used to seeing Sis. Simpson in a spiritual realm that I really didn't think of her as being human. Flesh and blood she was, and God, by His grace, let me see a glimpse of her human side. It was so precious to me. We, as a church, leaned on her so much that we often forgot that she had needs as well.

Prior to this, I always called Sis. Simpson for encouragement and uplifting; afterwards, I chose to encourage and uplift her. She was my friend, my confidant. God let me know that she needed one as well.

"Another precious moment for me was when I came to visit Sis. Simpson a few weeks before she died. On this particular day, I was reading chapters in Pslams to her and she fell asleep. I stayed with her and when she awoke, she told me they were outside. I couldn't understand who she said was outside. In my carnality, I asked her if it was the devil. Her eyes got real big, and she said, 'No, it was the angels.' It reminded me of when Richard and Doris Berford's baby was sick and how the angels would come to take little Stephen but would have to leave because of the faith that was permeated from prayer. The church at this time was praying and believing that God would raise her up and heal her. Their faith was so strong, it held the angels back until they were finally able to let her go. Prayer is an awesome thing!

"As a young teenager, I remember going to the church in the early morning hours to join Sis. Simpson in prayer. What a prayer warrior! She prayed for everyone calling out names and asking God to meet their needs. She was an awesome lady. God was her dearest friend, and she was His friend!

"I have experienced so many things in my life that have been a direct result of the influence Sis. Simpson had on my life. It would take another book to tell it all, so I find myself like Mary . . . pondering all in my heart."

Joan Cowan remembers . . .

"I remember when my son, Edward, had a bicycle wreck and the metal part of the pedal stuck into his leg just beneath the knee making a deep gash. As a very young saint, I wasn't quite sure what to do – take him to the doctor or not. I got my ID card and drove him to Sis. Simpson's for prayer. While we were praying for Edward the Lord spoke through Sis. Simpson, saying, 'I am the Lord God that heals thee.' Needless to say, I didn't take him to the doctor. I drove home, put a bandaid on it, and the Lord took care of the rest!

"Sis. Simpson was a wonderful woman. She radiated faith. She was a living example. When you saw the miraculous, supernatural, extraordinary things happening in and all around her life, she always gave God the honor. Everything she did was a reflection of him and not of her. That is why God could use her so mightily.

"Many times I have said, 'Follow Sis. Simpson as she follows Christ!' I am grateful that God allowed our lives to touch for a short time. I will never forget her or her teachings."

Bro. Philip Huffman was one of the young ministers that Sis. Simpson taught. He was killed in 1995. There were about 1500 people who signed the register at his  **funeral in the small community of Walnut, Mississippi. He was truly a servant of God and a shining example of her ministry.**

The following remembrance comes from Pastor Robert Barnett Jr., who purchased the church at 8190 Wilkinsville Road in Millington, Tennessee.

Pastor Robert Barnett remembers . . .

"A true woman and servant of God. The reason I stand today is because this woman of God stood in faith with me some 16 years ago. She taught me the real meaning of Romans 4:17, ' . . . and calleth those things that be not as though they were.' She prayed for me, that one day I would receive the baptism of the Holy Ghost, with the evidence of speaking with other tongues. I thank God today that because of her faith and prayers, I now enjoy the fulfillment of God's inner and outer power on my life. I'll always love and admire this anointed leader. "I'LL SEE YOU ON THE STREETS OF GLORY, PASTOR SIMPSON!"

(Pastor Robert Barnett Jr., The Living For Christ Church, 8190 Wilkinsville Rd., Millington, Tennessee)

Laurie Black remembers . . .

"About 19 1/2 years ago, I heard a dynamic speaker. She compelled me to seek God. In her church I received the Holy Ghost and was baptized in Jesus' Name. There I met my husband, and she married us. I speak of Sis. Simpson.

"Having moved to Memphis in May of 1984, my family began attending a church closer to our new home. Busy settling in, I didn't keep in touch with friends from the Millington United Pentecostal Church and was unaware of Sis. Simpson's failing health.

"Toward the end of August, I dreamed Sis. Simpson came to my bedroom. She stood before a large golden, oval-shaped mirror. She was dressed in white and wore a white veil. There was a sparkle in her eyes as she turned and walked toward me. 'Sis. Laurie, you just keep standing for God!' she said. 'Amos will come on back in, just stand for God! I'm going home now, you just stand for God!' She turned and was gone; so was the mirror.

"I woke shaken with tears running down my face. I looked at the clock; it was 4:00 a.m. It was too early to call anyone; so, I waited until 6:00 a.m. and called my friend, Vicki Keller. I told her of the dream. She then told me Sis. Simpson had cancer and was very ill. About a month later Sis. Simpson passed away. I was unable to attend her funeral, but I felt we had already said 'Good-bye.'

"I shall forever remember her with love. She changed my life and helped set my feet upon a different path. Praise God ! I love you Sis. Simpson."

LAST MINUTE BULLETIN:

At the time this book went to press, Shirley Armstrong, who was healed of a brain tumor, just underwent a second surgery for colon cancer. Tests showed two large tumors that had to be removed, and the doctors planned to do a colostomy. Prayer changes things! Not only could they not find the two tumors, they found Shirley's colon looking like a child's!

Not long after this, one of Shirley's doctors came to church to see the place where such miracles take place.

Hazel's God is still alive!

THE END

however, not totally, because
the story continues
with all of
us!

LET'S COMPARE
HAZEL WITH THE WOMAN
IN PROVERBS 31

•She was a virtuous woman. (Verse 10)

•Her husband safely trusted her. (Verse 11)

•She did him good all the days of her life. (Verse 12)

•She worked willingly with her hands. (Verse 13)

•She was like a merchants ship which brought her food from afar. (Verse 14) She prayed and brought manna from Heaven to her flock.

•She rose while it is yet night and gave meat to her household. (Verse l5) She arose at 5 a.m. went to church and prayed for this manna.

•She considered a field and bought it. (Verse 16) She bought 5 acres of land for the church. She planted vineyards for the Lord.

•She girded her loins with strength and strengthened her arms. (Verse 17) She strengtened herself and her church through prayer.

•She perceived that her merchandise was good and her candle went not out by night. (Verse 18) She prayed for her flock all hours of the night because they were good in her eyes.

•She layed her hands to the spindle for God. (Verse 19) She loved His work.

•She stretched out her hands to the poor and did many good things for them. (Verse 20)

•She was not afraid of the snow for her household. (Verse 21) She was not afraid the snow would warp those new beams that were exposed to the snow for six weeks when she was building the new church. She trusted God.

•She maketh herself coverings of tapestry. (Verse 22) She made crafts and crocheted things for her home and to sell for God's work also.

•Her clothing was silk and purple. (Verse 22)

•Her husband was known in the gates. (Verse 23)

•She maketh fine linen and selleth it. (Verse 24) The bible says the white linen is the righteousness of the saints. She preached God's word that purified his saints.

•Strength and honor were truly her clothing. (Verse 25)
She openeth her mouth with wisdom; and in her tongue was the law of kindness. (Verse 26) This perfectly discribes this handmaiden of the Lord.

•She looketh well to the ways of her household. (Verse 27) This she did in home and in her church. She ate not the bread of idleness.

•Her children rise up and call her blessed; her husband also praiseth her. (Verse 28) How true this was of Hazel.

•Many daughters have done virtuously but thou excellest them all. (Verse 29) Sister Hazel Simpson, this was true of YOU!

•Favor is deceitful and beauty is vain; but a woman that feareth the Lord, she shall be praised. (Verse 30) This God fearing lady shall live in the hearts of her children who praise her.

•Give her of the fruit of her hands, and her own works shall praise her. (verse 31)

She gave God all the glory!

ORDER FORM

Please send me _____ copies of **_"Hazel: God's Amazing Handmaiden."_** Enclosed is _____.
(\$9.95 plus \$1.50 shipping and handling for each book.)

SEND ORDER TO:

Freddie Turner
5041 Easley
Millington, TN 38053
901-872-1875

NAME_____

ADDRESS_____

CITY_____ STATE_____ ZIP_____

ORDER FORM

Please send me _____ copies of **_"Hazel: God's Amazing Handmaiden."_** Enclosed is _____.
(\$9.95 plus \$1.50 shipping and handling for each book.)

SEND ORDER TO:

Freddie Turner
5041 Easley
Millington, TN 38053
901-872-1875

NAME_____

ADDRESS_____

CITY_____ STATE_____ ZIP_____